Reddaren Academic Publishing

New York - London - Madrid - Paris - Hong Kong - Tokyo

All rights reserved. 2020. ISBN: 9798579568113

Reddaren Academic Publishing is committed to a sustainable future for our business, our readers, and our planet. This book is printed on demand and is available in electronic format.

Achieving for Nothing

Matt Stone

Introduction with random ideas

This book is going to be a continuous prologue describing my life experiences so far and the lessons I took from them, mixed with some other ideas. Why should this be of any interest for you? Because except for my name, which is a pseudonym to protect my identity and prevent my ego from interfering in my writing, everything else will be pure unaltered honesty. From me to you.

I am 37 years old at this moment, soon 38. I have come to the strange conclusion that I keep achieving things in life and they don't really mean anything in the end, so I decided to write a book with the few things I learned along the way. One could think that I am aiming for the wrong goals, but statistically speaking I have covered enough areas to invalidate that possibility altogether.

Take studies for example. I am a doctor (PhD). It hasn't changed anything relevant in my life. For some university positions and vacancies they would even prefer a master's degree actually. So it's something like this:

When I was watching the Indiana Jones movies and saw what Dr. Jones was doing and how he was regarded I couldn't help but thinking that, although exaggerated, there should be some degree of truth to the whole situation. Considered an expert in some field, secretive agencies interrupting your lectures to ask for your valuable take on some particular subject, and all that stuff. And here is where we find our first divergence. Let's go by these two ways at the same time. In the first way I quote you the statistics about how PhD holders earn more as an average occurrence and I complement this with a nice speech about how childish and pointless it would be to value achievements based on the money they produce or the way we are treated by fictional agents working in mysterious missions. The second way has a kid sitting there on a bench wondering why this achievement has left him as unfulfilled as many others before and after it. Those two ideas: at the same time. We are all fully capable of rationalizing those points and come up with explanations as to why it would be impossible to live in an Indiana Jones movie. The simplest approach would be to talk about the dissonance between the expectations created by movies and other cultural manifestations, after a while analyzing the phenomenon we would reach the conclusion that these formats and works are not descriptive but aspirational (meaning that the directors, writers, or actors of Indiana Jones don't live that type of life because it is an impossibility fueled by a convenient script and a plot armor). Then we could congratulate ourselves for finding the answer and look down on all those who take those movies, series, cartoons, anime, novels, etc. as a guide to shape their expectations of reality. But here is the problem with that approach: An endless intake of aspirational examples and stories has created a world of knights where all dragons have been slain and no one seems to have heard of castles, princesses... or where to find them.

It seems to be a worldwide phenomenon of our time. People adapt their abilities and expectations to a life that can't offer them the opportunities to shine and show their true potential. We lose as a society, as individuals, and as humanity. An example? We watch shows that talk about friendship and we identify our own limits in that regard, then we are thrown inside a reality where it's incredibly difficult to form those meaningful friendships that would allow us to realize our full human potential for friendship. On the other hand, this reality seems to be a never-ending source of pain and suffering... something that shouldn't still make us sad at this point of the reading, it's just a thread to pull from. Why is it so? There has to be some reason as to why pleasure is much more limited and difficult to find than suffering.

The first possibility is that humans, through our interactions and behaviors are creating conditions that are playing against us at an individual and collective level. That we are the ones to blame for the type of world we have created. The second possibility is that there is something intrinsic or foundational for the fact that life is providing us with so many opportunities for misery and fewer opportunities for happiness. Don't get me wrong... There will be plenty of time to raise our fists and shout at the skies above and all that, but right now we are just observing discrepancies in the balance between positive and negative. Losing a loved one to death, illness, circumstances, etc. seems to be much easier than gaining new loved ones due to similar circumstances and mechanisms of life. If everything were in perfect balance a very old person would die surrounded by a plethora of friends (a plethora, a big group... indulge me if I ever use weird words). I mean, in a statistically balanced reality a hypothetical old man would lose his best friend to some illness in his 50s, lose his wife in his 70s, etc. but would keep replenishing his circle of positive human beings near him at least to a basic balance where the number stays the same. But we can't forget that, theoretically speaking, humans would be tipping the scales since we invest time and energy searching for positive outcomes and avoiding negative ones. For example, we build hospitals where that hypothetical wife can fight against whatever condition is threatening to end her life. It's not as if we accept the negativity life throws our way without fighting or resisting, but even with all our might and capabilities fighting the bad and trying to improve the good in our lives, statistically speaking it is easier to find more old people dying alone than surrounded by the collection of new friends they keep building along their way through life. We could also rationalize this fact claiming that friendships and human relations are more complex than investing time and effort into trying to gain a positive outcome, but even with all the statistics about age, physical shape, social abilities, etc. taken into account we will need to agree that it is easier dying alone than surrounded by loving friends, a clue to the lack of balance in the primal mechanism that governs our reality.

The two possibilities we mentioned before: life being inherently tipped to get a bad result, and those bad results being circumstances produced by our own self-interests, could certainly be combined. It may be true that the number of situations and outcomes that we consider "positive" might be more limited than those we consider "negative". In certain areas like being healthy and ill it is clear to appreciate that when everything goes as it should regarding our health, we find ourselves in a neutral state, whereas when something goes wrong we find the negative side. Where would be the positive? After all, a heart beating normally, a body not aching, or a brain producing the hormones it should, are things that are expected and considered as normal. Therefore that would be the "neutral" state of things, and health problems would be "negative", but where would we find the "positive"? Our hearts working beyond their capabilities? Gaining superpowers? When could we claim that we have surpassed the "neutral" functioning of an organ or limb? The statement: "My arms are still attached to my body and they don't ache!" is hardly a positive circumstance but something neutral and expected from those particular parts of the body.

So even if we agree that positive and negative outcomes are subjective and could be defined in many ways according to our own opinions, when we look at the cold facts of objective examples it is much simpler to tell a negative apart from a neutral situation than to tell when or where a positive outcome is happening or being produced.

So the first objective truth we can take from these observations is that if we want positive outcomes we need to work hard for them since, statistically speaking, it is easier to get a neutral result or a negative one if we don't put effort and planning into things.

The idea that even if you achieve the positive outcome you wanted, you can still be left unfulfilled and wondering what is life all about... is perhaps one of the worst tests of character we need to face in this reality of ours. Again, it's not about unrealistic expectations, but about the strange idea that you reached the end of a race where there are no trophies, medals, or consequences for winning. You look around and ask: "Where do I go from here? Shouldn't something happen now?" The idea that there is no way to run is perhaps more terrifying than not knowing if you will finish the race or not. You could finish it, and nothing would change, and that's a grim prospect.

Another good example for this trend are martial arts. Any sport in general would be valid actually. After dedicating your life to something and being good at it, coming to the realization that your life is mostly about running fast, or throwing a ball through a hoop, or moving in a pool of water faster than others... could make us question the roads we took, the goals we thought we wanted to achieve, and their value in our deep development as human beings. Those activities have good effects on the body, they produce money if we are good enough at them, etc. but they may leave us lacking a true purpose in life. A higher one. A medical doctor might also make money and enjoy what he does but at the end of the day whenever he has a moment of introspection and self-reflection he will realize that from an objective point of view, saving lives through operations or good medical decisions is something that brings deeper value and fulfillment than just running fast to entertain people. I am not saying that any other activity that is not medicine is devoid of value or fulfillment. If that were the case I, myself, would have studied medicine instead of history, philosophy, and all the other stuff.

The point I am trying to make is that if our job or main activity doesn't provide us with deep existential meaning or with a sense of fulfillment, we may be interested in finding those two things extending our range of action or choosing secondary activities to find balance. For example, swimming is fun and teaching others how to swim can allow them to have fun or even take them out of a dangerous situation one day. Not only helping others can give us a sense of meaning and existential peace in my opinion. Improving ourselves can also do the trick, but it can also leave us wondering if that's the correct way. Imagine learning Russian or Chinese for a few years only to discover that we are denied a visa to those countries, or that after visiting we don't really like them... The value of the time and energy invested would certainly decrease in those circumstance, even if we all understand the basic idea that any improvement is good, learning a language that you no longer plan to use as much as before might also create this idea that we chose the wrong way to go.

The same happens with martial arts. I have trained different things since I was 7 years old. Judo, Karate, Kickboxing, Aikido, Kung Fu, Jujutsu, etc. I have gone from one to the next acquiring different black belts and titles along the way. This could be seen as me boasting if it weren't for the fact that as the years go by it feels more and more like a never-ending quest that might not even provide me with worthy results. I can't help but realize that all the movie stars I was idolizing as a teenager when I was training hard are now looking really bad. And yes, we can all come up with rational arguments about drug use, alcoholism, age taking a toll, and all that other stuff... The reality is that one way or another with physical activities and martial arts in particular, the more you train the less results you will achieve when you factor in time and body degradation. Again, yes, it's better to train and to know martial arts than not doing those two things, it's not about that, but about the fact that your efforts and dedication will be granting you less and less results as you move into your 50s, 60s, 70s, etc. until we finally die. And again, we all understand that it is something natural, and that's how life is, and what are we gonna do about it and blah, blah... but that doesn't make it less disheartening: "I am 25 years old now, if I train another 25 years maybe I can compete in the Olympics!" Errr... no... it doesn't matter how hard you train, few sports will allow you to take part in the Olympics when you are 50. It doesn't depend on you or the time or passion you put into your training. Is this message depressing? Not really... It's a bit sad but that's all. I guess the lesson we should take from this would be to not become obsessed with a sport and activity beyond its logical benefits and positive effects. Overdoing something will burn us out, produce injuries, mental stress, etc. and the positive effects will not increase based on our extra time and passion dedicated to the activity.

Let's go with a simple example to illustrate this last thought. We all tie our shoes moderately well, right? Well what if I told you that there is a secret temple in Tibet where if you study 7 years in a secluded mountain you could increase the results of your shoe-tying abilities by 20%? We would all probably think that even though achieving a better result at something is positive, it doesn't compensate for the time and effort we would need to invest to gain that little extra benefit in performance. This way of thinking can be applied to many other activities and personal relations measuring the connection between effort invested and outcome obtained. Not everything in life has to be done perfectly, and not every price is fair for an improvement in performance or skill. And again, I am not saying that no activity is worth doing at our maximum capacity and with absolute dedication. We already discussed before how some activities will bring us a deeper meaning and the investment may be worth it. Perhaps we wouldn't go for 7 years to a temple to improve the way in which we tie our shoes, but we would go 7 years to some institution, club, or school that provides us with the knowledge that we require to build houses, understand law, learn philosophy, or something like that.

Is the message of this long prologue that we should go through life in an apathetic way doing things half-heartedly because anyway we will get old and die one day? No... Certainly not. I was aiming at explaining how the dynamics between passion, time, and energy dedicated to some goal need to be accurately calibrated with the real benefits we would obtain from them.

CHAPTER ONE: Childhood Timelines and Forgery

Unusual ideas, unusual experiences... just like you've read so far. First of all I was bullied and a bully at different moments of my student life. I remember the environment at my school like a playing field where you were supposed to answer back if someone tried to put you down or belittle you in any way. With that thought in mind I remember a fat kid who was laughing at me probably in an effort to feel better about himself or something. I got offended that he thought I would be a good target to mess with, so I went from positive-neutral to chaotic evil in the blink of an eye. I was drawing him in art class in the least favorable way, showing the drawing around while laughing at his face, teeth, weight... In my mind I felt I was correcting an evil that had been inflicted upon me... I was young and stupid enough to think that I was right in doing what I was doing, and perhaps the first two or three answers to his actions were justified, but I went on and on to the point where I would create the most convoluted situations still thinking that I was bringing balance to the universe or teaching him a lesson or something like that. I wasn't... That lesson had been learned days ago and at this point I was just crossing line after line acting like a real jerk and entering evil territory little by little. Until one day I thought there would be a fight between us, but there wasn't. I went incredibly far with my comments and jokes and he started crying in his desk. I had never felt so ashamed of myself before, so it was like a sudden realization. I had gone so far in my righteous lust for retribution that I had become an evil bully myself.

The next day I apologized profusely and little by little we became good friends, to the point where we were companions in school strips and stuff like that. This would have been a warm story if it weren't for the fact that a couple years later when he saw the opportunity to seem cool again by laughing at someone to deflect the laughs away from himself, he picked me again, convinced that I wouldn't retaliate this time after our friendship had been formed. I did retaliate, but much less than before, and our friendship ended having granted me two important lessons. The first one was that I could be right all along... step by step right until the moment where I cross the line and become evil. There is no in-between before one goes too far and goes from hero to villain in the blink of an eye. I guess that was the moment when I decided to be careful in the type of reactions I give towards other people's actions because they could really be the cause of my ethical demise.

The second lesson has a lot to do with friendship and character. Someone who would try to put others down to not be the target himself is likely to throw you under the bus whenever the circumstances make it seem like a sensible choice in the future. It's a character flaw, and as much as we are supposed to consider mercy, second chances, and all that, we should also remember that unless there is a catharsis or a process of growth, the same character flaws that made a person act a certain way will probably take them down that road in the future. A simple apology is unlikely to change a trait deeply rooted in someone's personality, so I try to look for that catharsis or "aha" moment in others before giving second chances for character flaws. A theory that even I myself would prove right in the future, because I went too far retaliating against bullies a couple more times... I was a slow learner apparently, and retaliation was indeed deeply rooted in my character.

Fast forward a few years, I was 15, not one year more, not one year less. People at my high school knew that I was somewhat well-trained in martial arts, so they kept their distance, but this was a private high school filled with kids from broken homes and weird environments that bordered criminality openly. My dad had died when I was 12 and my mom thought it would be good to go from a private school to a public high school to meet other kinds of people and open my horizons and what not. I was for a year and a half in constant shock (until I dropped out, but more on that later, and don't worry... that story ends well and with a PhD as you already know). Guys carrying knives, stealing from the teachers' purses in the corridors or if they left the classroom for a second, chairs and tables being thrown out of the windows of a third floor without looking down to see if someone is passing by... It was a cesspool of uncivilized madness from the worst examples that this particular society had to offer. I tried being myself instead of toughening up confident in the knowledge that I would win any fight with my martial skills, but oh... as soon as they understood how the game of martial arts was played back then, they saw an opening in my defenses. You see, you were not supposed to initiate the fights yourself. You are supposed to defend from clear aggressions and to have a strong and compelling reason to break someone's nose. That was half of my thinking process, the other half was that my mom had lost my dad recently and every time I would mention casually my problems in that high school of nightmares she would start getting worried and begging me not to hurt anyone or do something that could spoil my life. A couple of years earlier she had seen me breaking someone's nose for pushing me while I was passing by him, and after two more years of training she got the idea that I could hurt some student badly if I fought against them. So with both of those circumstances in action, there were instances where there would be insults, comments, a piece of chalk being thrown your way, and that type of stuff that would get on your nerves, but wouldn't be enough to start a fight. Those kids were experts in moving inside that grey area where I had no resources to fight back very well.

There was one particular bully who understood that perfectly. So one day after many bitchy comments and insulting jokes I approached him and said: "I got enough of your shit. Come here. Let's fight". With a smile on his face he said something like: "Nah. I wouldn't win", and I called him a coward in front of all the other classmates, smiled, and I went down the stairs thinking in my naive logic that this was the end of it. In the afternoon classes again the same bitchy comments and again inside this area where if you answered back you wouldn't get anything, and if you punched him in the face you would get expelled or criminal charges depending on what you did to him. It was fascinating to me that you could throw a chair down a third floor or bring weapons to a public building without thinking of the consequences, but if you broke someone's nose it would be a horrible crime against humanity or something. I am telling you kids... the 90s were crazy. There was a question from my mom that would haunt me for a few days, showing me my limitations: "with all the things you trained, can't you do anything to them besides punching them in the face?" Well... up until that point I had trained Full Contact, Kickboxing, and Karate. I could punch them, kick them, punch them and kick them at the same time, hit them with the elbows... Yep, that was all. I had no resources or tools in my arsenal to start a fight without being the aggressor. After that I saw the importance of paying attention to things I had considered useless up until that point like joint locks, evasive movements, control techniques, etc. I honestly thought I could solve any violent situation punching or kicking someone in the face. It didn't even cross my mind that living in a civilized society I might want to benefit from the possibility of not having to brutally destroy someone's face or internal organs as soon as there was a chance for a physical confrontation. I checked my options and realized the only sensible thing I could do was to quit that high school mid-term and try somewhere else. Surprisingly, my mom was happy about me leaving that situation without hurting anyone. Her happiness about me not having serious troubles surpassed her worries for my academic future. Priorities I guess. She had spoken with the principal a few times even warning him about my training and personal situation. The guy was the type of bureaucrat who stared blankly at you with empty eyes and couldn't care less about anything that didn't put his job in jeopardy or forced him to adhere to some protocol. Back then a student breaking someone's face would have prompted a response, but mean comments and constant insulting jokes wouldn't. There wasn't a lot of awareness about bullying back then, and the phrase: "my kickboxing expert son is being bullied" didn't really attract a lot of empathy.

Anyway, that has to be the most pathetic and unfulfilling high school bullying story ever. I can't really offer you anything satisfying regarding that bully, nor can I say that I was the typical victim of bullying. I broke someone's nose for pushing me on the street, my mom saw it walking a few steps ahead of me, and since then all her efforts were about trying to prevent me from hurting someone badly. Given our family situation I didn't want to upset her or see her worried and I saw no better alternative than quitting even when confronting your bully and challenging him to a fight would produce no results at all. Sitting now here, or rather, kneeling on some folded blankets as I type because my table is really low, I wonder if I should have started that fight with some push, or some light slap and a smile or so... Now at this age I see other possibilities and I have other resources, but there is no guarantee that at 15 I wouldn't have punched that guy over and over because I really hated him. Given all the circumstances and limitations I still see no safer option than what I did. I quit that place and started writing my future plans in a notebook. A habit that has made me see clearer paths for my future since then, but more on that habit later... Anyway, worst bullied kid ever...

Well there is one thing... After a few years, when I was 19 I had a period when I stopped worrying about the consequences for some time. Now I am back to my careful and sensible self, but at that time I remember not taking any crap from anyone. "So what if there is a fight and I hurt someone? I will think of something to get away from the consequences. The street is not a high school where they know your name, after all". I had lost my hair at 18 due to an excess of testosterone according to the doctors, and some guy on the street was asking some old ladies for money. He was being extremely polite to them, but when I passed by he shouted: "Hey! You! Baldy! Come here!" I turned around with my fist ready to punch him, and advanced a few steps. The guy must have read the situation very well because he started apologizing and saying it was just a friendly way to refer to me, and that it looked really good. The episode would be irrelevant unless for that voice inside you that tells you: "are you gonna let him speak to you like that? Punch him... Show him a lesson!" And sensible as I had been in high school that other time, this time I was ready to use violence at the slightest provocation, but was able to contain myself.

Coming back to the title of the chapter, I always found it interesting to think of the possibilities that get lost in an ocean of multiverses because of people making stupid choices. Your 30s are an age where you already had the chance to see the girls you liked in school, high school, university, etc. make the wrong choices so you see these beautiful creatures with all their potential for being happy and giving happiness wasted, and it makes you wonder about the different versions of reality in which they made the right choices. Smoking or not smoking? Well, one of those two will make your teeth black and spoil your internal organs, the other will not: you be the judge on which alternative should be picked for optimal results and then wonder why we still have smokers in this day and age. Personal freedom is great for human development and all that, but the idea of different realities where things took a different turn is really appealing. Like: "No... Instead of dating that abusive guy who treats you like shit to subconsciously punish yourself for crimes you didn't commit, if you had dated my friend who was more handsome, smarter, and treated you better, we could all have gone to the lake to swim and play volleyball while we tell jokes, and have fun making awesome moments for everyone to enjoy. But no, after a life of making the wrong choices you contact me on social media to ask about my friend, the handsome one who would have made you happier than the shitty partner you picked, and I have to tell you that he spent two years daydreaming about you, that he finally gave up and found a girl that makes him happy, and you tell me about the life of drama and sadness that you picked for yourself, I ask you about the kid in your pictures, you explain me how difficult it is to be a single mother, I pretend to listen, and the conversation ends with a sharp pain for the wasted possibilities we could have lived, and the beautiful moments that never were.

A bit too dramatic perhaps, I know, but don't tell me you don't get a similar feeling when you see so much wasted human potential. Life already makes it difficult enough for us to find happiness without having to factor in our own dumb choices regarding health, partners, habits... It would be cool if after we die we were given an explanation of everything that we didn't know was going on, like: "Welcome! Well in the first scene you can see that the girl that was cold to you at school and pretended to ignore you, but she actually liked you a lot and wrote your name inside hearts, she was just following bad advice from her mom who insisted that showing interest made men like girls less... Yes, the mom was dumb for not knowing about different personality types, the daughter was dumb for following her advice, you were dumb for never noticing how she was looking at you when you spoke in a class or played with friends during the recess... And here is a version of that same reality where things are done right, and you two have your first kiss, and this is the part where you roll around in the grass of that park near your school, and you caress her face and you tell her that you love her, and she feels happy that you told her you feel the same way she had been feeling for you for a long time. You don't marry or live happily ever after because you are just a couple of kids, but those warm memories of how loving and being loved should feel like are a guide that prevents you from being hurt in future relationships. It makes you both realize you have the ability to love deeply, and that you are worthy of being loved as well. A beautiful love of youth".

The general idea is that the world could be a better place with the right habits and functioning mechanisms put in place. You can see some of those examples in specific groups of people doing specific activities. The overwhelming majority of nature enthusiasts and travelers that I have met were positive and helpful. Likewise, the general trend among military people is to care about others and to be courteous. It's hard to meet a stressed surfer, or angry bakers. I am not saying that somehow practicing these activities shields us from being selfish, negative, or harmful to others or to ourselves, but there is some statistical truth in the fact some activities and attitudes produce more positive results in us.

Coming back to my childhood memories for a while, quitting high school was a very scary experience. Everyone around me was either laughing at me or feeling pity for the situation of the poor teenager who loses his father and starts acting up spoiling a promising academic career. I have to say that at the time, the opinions and points of view of those people made me doubt my decision very much. It's natural and even good that we can listen to external points of view to contrast those with our own. I am personally very far from the idea that ignoring everything everyone else has to say is the right path to live your life in the best possible way. I take information and opinions from other people all the time, from books they wrote, conversations we had, questions in forums, etc. It seems very obvious having to explain this, but as in other areas of life I like to have a balance between doing things my own way and outright ignoring everything everyone else has to say about any topic.

Since I couldn't be transferred that academic year to another high school, I spent months analyzing different programs, possibilities, subjects, technical schools, etc. If I could go back in time I would probably advise my younger self to pursue vocational training related with administrative skills. That would have been practical and with a wide range of possibilities to choose from in terms of employment. Instead I got myself in an external marketing program from some school collaborating with a university. I liked marketing a lot, I still do, but following that particular passion was expensive and not very practical. I got my certificate after months of tests, but then again... everyone does. It's kinda difficult to fail in one of those courses you have to pay yourself. It was a mistake and a waste of time. Nobody would have hired a 16-year-old marketing specialist for anything, and that type of education was only good to make your CV more presentable, not to be the base for future development. Just so that you can see how badly I miscalculated that particular move, I had asked for a computer with internet connection and for that marketing program at the same time. We only had money for one of those two things at home, and I chose the marketing program. Let that sink in... Instead of entering the magical world of Internet in 1999 when everything was starting and I could have had loads of opportunities available, I got a piece of paper saying I was a 16-year-old marketing specialist. Brilliant move.

After months of doing things my way I realized I couldn't go very far. The vocational and professional programs in my city were either too far away, too difficult, too expensive, or too full of people to accommodate me that academic year. I thought the system had cheated me, I saw nothing but dead ends and fake doors like those on video games... you know... the ones you approach and realize: "oh, this is just painted on the wall, it's not a real door that can be opened". So I got frustrated and began acting weird, but in a respectful way. What I mean is that I wasn't taking drugs, breaking the house with a hammer, or cursing at anyone... I started going to sleep later and later until I purposefully started living at night for at least three months. I would watch programs in different languages, read all the books in the house, acquire more, and write plans in several notebooks. It wasn't anything like a comeback or rising from the ashes, or anything like that. I was anxious and sad about the way my life had turned out to be. I was wondering over and over why was it necessary for my life story that I had lost my father so early. I often wondered if he would have given me some advice or some help, had the circumstances been different. It caused me some discomfort to look around me and see everyone else seemed to be doing fine with their dad and mom. Even the children from divorced parents could still get help or guidance if they needed that at some point. In my whole school there were only two other kids without a father, so I always thought it as a statistical anomaly when I became the third. Of the other two kids, one had quite a big family that could soften that blow a bit, difficult as it may have been for him too. The other one also had an extended family I think, but he was the typical kid who would take his anger out on others. We had some sort of a bonding conversation after my dad's funeral. It went more or less like this:

-Rebel kid: "Hey, sorry about your dad. You seem to be doing fine though"
-Me: "No, not really. But, there's nothing I can do about it"
-Rebel kid: -visibly taken aback- "Uh! You are a tough guy then, aren't you?"
-Me: "Nah, I don't think so"

He left to do his things looking back a couple of times with some sort of empty smile. It would have been hard for 12-year-old me to explain him that destroying public property or scaring old ladies with firecrackers would do little to bring my dad back, and it would have probably made him ashamed of me. As a kid I felt some sort of responsibility for it, as if his death meant that I had to become more responsible myself, and to try not to cause more troubles to a broken family consisting now of three people, including myself. Up until that point I had never payed attention whenever I saw a happy family doing happy family stuff. As the months went by I would catch myself more and more often looking at some window where there was a birthday, or some nice family moment happening. I wasn't looking at them with envy or any negative emotions. They were a warm reminder of how things should be, but weren't. The only thoughts in my mind was something among the lines of: "Why not me?" "Why did this have to happen to me when the majority of people seem to be having a usual life story?"

The sense of responsibility gave way with the years to a sharp reproach. My dad had died of lung cancer and I would often catch myself blaming him for smoking. It would be something like: "Wow, I sure hope those cigarettes felt good day after day... You left us alone here. Well done, man... Poisoning yourself with that shit until you finally died". I often dreamed about having my dad in my life. In my dreams everything was normal and we were in usual situations, but after waking up the feeling of betrayal and being cheated by life came back. I began to resent having to teach myself how to shave, having to fight all my battles alone, and not having another man in the house to understand me the way he had done up until I was twelve. I can honestly say that among the worst things of that situation was the fact that I felt more and more alone in an apartment with my mom and my older sister. At a time when I would have needed manly activities and father-son time I got obnoxious gossip programs and an overall feminization of the environment I was living in. I mostly spent time in my room, but it was the smallest in a 62 sq. meter (665 sq. ft.) apartment so when I saw Harry Potter living under the stairs I felt his pain as mine. My room didn't even have four walls... I am not making this up... It's one of those space designs where the living room is joined with this other smaller room and there is a sliding panel door separating both spaces. So now you see why those months I spent living at night when the house was silent and without gossip programs were so much needed for my sanity at the time.

For the small minority of readers thinking: "Oh, losing your dad is always sad, but surely you could recover from that in a few years, right?" Yes, yes... In normal circumstances you would be right, but my life story defies the statistics with alarming odds. When I was 22 my mom died. It was also cancer, but due to menopause complications rather than anything directly attributed to her life habits. Now, I am not saying that my life is the saddest you will ever see... But the comparison with the average person seems to go in their favor. The other day I had a brief chat with a neighbor from my block of apartments. She was complaining about not being able to see her parents due some health restrictions coming after the covid-19 virus (check it out if you are reading this book long after 2020, you will honestly begin to think that the humans living in those years were cursed or something). Anyhow, I stared at this lady in her 60s, complaining about not being able to see her parents in her 80s for a few weeks already, and I smiled politely, and I wished her with total honesty that the situation improves soon... All while wondering why my life deviates so much from hers in terms of number of parents available and years enjoyed with them. In situations like those it feels like some of us are playing the game of life with difficult settings instead of the regular usual ones.

This is as good a moment as any other to remind you that there is a difference between pointless complaining and a healthy and necessary observation of the facts and statistics to determine whether we are right or wrong in thinking that life is perhaps a bit harder for some than for others. It is healthy in the way that sometimes we can catch ourselves wondering if perhaps we are being too dramatic, or even crybabies at some point. It's good to sit down and review the circumstances to know where we stand. Yes, we can always do activities that bring our mood up, we can always discover new things and places, we can always be positive and dynamic pursuing happiness, but there is no point in denying the reality that some of our lives are more difficult than the average one. It's not something to throw at their faces from our pedestal of vital superiority, but rather a nice reminder that external complications should also be taken into account when analyzing our lives and personal situations.

Anyway... Coming back to the point in which I was unable to go on with my studies and I had acquired a useless marketing certificate instead of a computer with internet (it is painful to read it, I know). I felt myself cheated and deceived by life, by the system, by something outside my control... so I leaned on the dark side for a while, within the bounds of ethics because I didn't hurt anyone or destroy anything, but far away from morals because I planned how to cheat the system back.

I looked at the booklet with my qualifications from high school and explored the pages. It finished abruptly in the middle. I came up with a weird idea that consisted on finishing the rest of the pages myself to be able to go through the last year remotely. Distance learning for high school stuff was easier because they assumed that option was for kids who lived in faraway villages of 20 people or so. There was also this belief that if you are doing high school that way it might be because you are trying to turn your life around after going to jail, or trying to fulfill a lifelong dream after retirement, or any of that stuff. So basically the study programs had changed recently and were now easier, plus the extra push you would get from finishing your studies through distance learning... it was much easier to pass the last year that way without having to study too much.

Part of my plan consisted on making it seem as if I was re-taking the last year but had already passed the difficult subjects. The only ones left were English, Spanish, Philosophy, etc. I picked the easiest possible route and further removed hurdles like Latin, Physics, Math, etc. pretending I had already passed them the year before.

I went to a big stationary in my city and got the type of sticking paper I needed for the pages, I designed the stickers using computers at an internet café, and emailed myself the results since one could not plug a USB memory in those computers. I printed the word document on the stickers at another place and I was half-way through my plan. I gave myself low scores on everything so that it would look even less suspicious... Who would go through all that trouble to give themselves such mediocre scores?

Now came the difficult part. The high school I had quit had my files and their seal was quite specific. Besides that, someone

could check one page and the next and see there was a difference
in the seals (the rubber stamps they use to validate the pages
after passing each year). I decided it would be wiser to claim I
quit one high school and got transferred to a different one that
was bigger and would make it more believable if they didn't have
me on their files. All this caution was an overkill on my part,
since the distance learning high school program only checked the
photocopy of my transcripts and didn't care about anything else.
But unaware of these facts about public bureaucracy at the time
I proceeded as if the authorities were on my tail and about to
send document experts or some stuff.

I went to one printing place next to the high school I was
pretending to have studied at and the conversation went along
these lines:

Me: -Hi, I need a rubber stamp that says "------- High School,
Name of the city"
Guy at the counter: *raises an eyebrow*
Me: And a big smiley face in the middle... It's for the school
newspaper. We will be stamping new submissions and stuff.
Guy at the counter: -Ah... Ok... What smiley face do you want?
We have several available
Me: Er... That one! Thanks.

I waited for the rubber stamp to be made, inside the shop.
Looking at the whole process and chatting with the guy to make
sure he wouldn't call the high school or some stuff. Again... I was
being paranoid because there is no law against writing the name
of a high school and a city in a rubber stamp or anything like
that. When the item was finished I went to a second printing
place faraway from this one and I asked for a seal with the coat
of arms of my region. The guy was curious about my motivations
and the conversation went like this:

Me: Yes, a stamp with the coat of arms of the region.
Guy: What for? I mean, why such a design?
Me: We are playing board games with people from other regions
and we want to stamp our letters and papers with the coat of

arms of the region, so that they know where we come from.
Guy: Oh... what size do you want?
Me (thinking): *Any size that fits the other stamp once I remove the smiley face with a razor*

I combined both rubber stamps together and went on to stick the papers in my booklet and to do everything properly. I also needed some signatures on a rubber stamp... back then it seemed to be fashionable that teachers left that thing at the secretary's office so they didn't have to sign all those booklets themselves by hand. Those rubber stamps were the easiest and I was in the clear. I asked my mom to do two of the signatures after explaining her my weird plans. When she saw the booklet covered and the pages I had made being identical to the real ones preceding them, she started laughing and understood that I had managed to come up with an ingenious way to finish my education. I wasn't causing any harm to anyone, the positions at the distance learning program weren't limited or anything like that. The perfect crime.

I finished the last year and graduated without too many problems. My scores were low due to the ones I had given myself and the ones I had got for real so, my career choices were limited to Humanities (excluding Law and Psychology, but surprisingly including Anthropology... nobody wanted to be an anthropologist in those days so they accepted anyone). But instead of using this opportunity to finally get on with the program and go to university in one of those degrees without any limitations for entry, I became bold and decided to go to London because I had some relatives there that had been constantly inviting me to come.

The lessons I took from all this were many. All the time I had lost quitting high school was given back to me with a few stickers and a rubber stamp. It made me have impostor syndrome for some time. I still think even nowadays if I am really an impostor... If someone could start digging and realize I cheated in high school and therefore I shouldn't have been allowed to enter a university. I have no idea how those two things connect, but the impostor syndrome went away when I accepted that I was in fact a cheater and consciously did my best to look like a "real" university student, and then a "real" teacher, and then a "real" university lecturer.

CHAPTER TWO: London, Studies, and Stocks

I had always had the dream of investing money in stocks. At home they used to buy the newspaper the last day of the year to cut the pages of stocks because you could see the minimum and maximum price for each company that year. Then I would compare them and write the averages and the maximums and minimums by hand and try to choose the right companies. All this in my mind, of course... We didn't have money for me to invest for real, but I had made around 15% of imaginary money and I went around claiming I could do the same with real money. So the next step was going to London to those relatives and extend my welcome as much as possible while I made some cash working temporary jobs.

I saved for having pocket money there by controlling some of the things I was consuming. Sometimes when I review the financial situation of the family back then I have the feeling that we could have been in a much better position had we planned things right for some time. I started taking care of part of my food expenses to pocket the difference. Particularly cookies, chocolate, sweets, money for going out, arcade coins, etc. I would limit the amount of those things that I bought while keeping a balance with my needs to make it look like life was still normal in those months previous to my trip. Buddies and I would go to the arcade to play video games and I would choose only those in which I was good at to last longer with one coin. Some days I would look how my friends played and treasure the couple of coins I had saved that afternoon. Cutting corners like a crazy person I managed to save the equivalent of money I would need for a gaming console and a few games. The temptation to buy one was there, but I knew that traveling to some new city without a financial safety cushion would increase my chances of failing at the whole thing. My older cousin and his family came on holidays to my city, and then we left together for London, where they lived.

I can't begin to describe you how out of my league I was at 17 in one of the biggest capitals in the world. I got fired from my first job for not understanding how the slips where you put your hours worked. You see, my first work day had been a Friday, they had told me to get the paper signed just because it was the end of the working week for us. I thought I was supposed to get it signed every day, so on Monday after my working day carrying boxes and helping some handyman with his tasks, I went to my boss and asked her to sign my paper. Apparently that meant that I was quitting... It was as if saying: "this is my last working day this week, so sign this". Nobody bothered to explain me how that stuff worked. I am sure London has become a paradise of joyful love and patient understanding towards teenage immigrants who go there to perform menial jobs, but at the time I was met with a: "we will miss you, bye" that I didn't really understand within that context, and I was told by the temp agency that same afternoon that I had actually quit my job without knowing it and that I was too stupid to work with them carrying boxes... Well, they didn't say it like that because they had that fake indirect way of talking in that particular city, at that particular time.

The next days I went up and down London burning my pocket money in travel cards and snacks hoping to find some more work. My cousin helped me with all this, but there was a change of attitude that is worth mentioning. I had been used to welcoming that kid in my city every two or three years and he was the foreigner who didn't know anyone and barely spoke the language (big hint to know that English is not my native language). Playing with him, taking him shopping, seeing him getting ripped off when he insisted on buying from street stands outside the stadium with his thick accent... It was a dynamic in which I had to take care of my cousin, or at least do everything to make him feel integrated and all that. I liked that. But now I was the younger cousin in a totally new place. I didn't understand half of what his friends were saying in their cockney accents, and I was out of the conversation most of the time. Now that the situation was the opposite, I quickly became a drag. It made me think how circumstances could affect human relations. My silent and shy cousin who had to be taken to places almost by the hand in my country, was now the one who had to take me here and there through all the bureaucratic problems of an immigrant:

Me: -Hi! I would like to open a bank account please.
Clerk: -The minimum deposit is 1,500 pounds.
Me: -Oh no, I need the bank account to get paid by the temp agency. I can't say I go around carrying that amount of cash with me.
Clerk: -Sorry... Can't help you.
Cousin: *sigh* Don't worry, they can pay you through my account, let's go.
Me: Damn... What would I do if I were alone in this crazy place? Coming all this way just to find out you need to have all that cash with you to open an account, and the temp agency doesn't want to pay you in any other way. Bureaucratic checkmate and back home feeling like a failure. Thanks cousin!

In my second job there were two guys from Jamaica. One was funny and the other one was a psycho who got verbally abusive with everyone there and got fired. The cool one was Winston. I must have asked him 4 or 5 times about Patois but I always forgot his answers. The conversations at that place were bizarre, but they also told you a lot about people and their priorities, cultural limitations, etc. Every payday we would discuss what we would do with the money. The nice girl from Cameroon always mentioned buying some boots, clothes, etc. The French guy from Normandy planned to have some fun on the weekend. Winston and I were the ones saving like little ants preparing for the winter. I guess that saving mentality is difficult to explain to others who don't already have that instinct, because for people who save money it just makes sense instinctively. You see the propensity that life has for screwing you over and you think: "Hey, I don't trust you, life... let me try to be ready for the next time you decide to give me unemployment, or a crisis, or a super-virus, or a typhoon made of crocodiles or something..." whereas for other people it's like: "wow! With this paycheck you could rent a big house in my country for half a month!" And after those fifteen days the Lord will provide for them or something like that... whereas for those with a saving mentality it's more like: "let me try to guess the next huge hurdle life will throw at me and also how much from my savings will I need to stay afloat".

In London I was picking boxes, unpacking clothes, packing postcards to send them to the shops, I was working in an old shopping mall in the center, at a Sainsbury's supermarket, handing out flyers... Those two days with the flyers were funny. I was in a team with a black guy who found it fascinating to have a white foreign guy in his car. We had to go to different spots and he would do everything possible to insert other activities in between so he could introduce me to his friends, to the owners of the shops he visited, etc. Our conversations were culturally enriching. It was the first time my saving mentality got challenged to the point of defeat:

Him: I am saving for a gold necklace.
Me: Why would you want to spend money on jewelry?
Him: It's cool. It gives you some style, you know?
Me: I dunno... I don't imagine myself saving up for stuff like that.
Him: It gets the girls' attention here. They notice you much more.
Me: Oh... Where do you say they sell these necklaces?

I didn't buy one because some items only look good if you tick certain boxes and possess particular characteristics. A pipe looks cool for an 80-year-old sailor, lingerie looks cool for young girls, and those two items and situations are not interchangeable, unfair as that may be. This reminds me that I had a very strange attitude in London that perhaps still drags me down a bit to this day. I was fine interacting with people and being friendly, but I was never bold enough to propose them to keep in contact after the job was done. I wasn't keen on accepting invitations to unknown places either, which is probably wise and sensible when you are a teenage kid in a big city, but it may also make you lose some opportunities for fun and nice experiences I guess.

Pros of caution when letting people close to you: You don't get raped or stabbed in an alley quite as often.
Cons: You spend months in London and you only go to parks, museums, and stuff like that... I think I visited a disco or a pub less than 10 times in all those months. I had a few excuses on my side though. I don't drink alcohol (I hate the taste, that's all... nothing deep about it), we got the attention of a group of girls the second night we went out to a disco, somebody told them I was still 17 at the time to sabotage me, and it spoiled my night. After that I thought something along the lines of: "Look... I don't drink anything in those places, it is unlikely that I can get girls being younger than them (18 was the minimum age to enter, but the bouncer looked the other way if you seemed presentable), and I have music at home... I better focus on improving my English and working to save money".

I spent New Year alone there. I had fun because of the TV programs in different channels, the food I bought for my special dinner, the music I was playing, the house for myself with adult movies... Again, it's probably one of those personality traits that come with you in the initial package. If you have a high score in introvert points you start adding up the cool food, the entertainment, the calm surrounding, and your thoughts of "uh, look at me... alone in New Year. I am a poor victim of a game I did not create nor understand how to play" and you suddenly feel better than if you were in some place surrounded by strangers, unable to control the music, or get anything you require from the situation. Like a pig rolling around in the mud of going your own personal way and doing your own thing instead of falling in line. That habit can also be problematic if I can't find the right balance for it, because saying NO to every possibility for fun and new experiences just because of how cool it is to be by yourself doing your own thing would make me miss a lot of interesting things, I guess.

Be it as it may... I came back to my country with some savings, less hair, and the strange feeling that the London I had been living in was not the one from the stories of my father or other relatives who had gone there looking for some foreign experience and a bit of adventure. It was quite fashionable in the 70s, 80s, and 90s. The stories were all the same, about nice polite gentlemen wearing funny hats and showing their good manners at the slightest chance. Already back then in 2000 and 2001 you could hear stories from my own relatives and from visitors and average Londoners about how the city had changed with time. While I was there I heard shots a couple of times, I saw a few fights (one of them with knives), and my uncle got attacked with a stick one day on his way to the metro station to steal his travel card and pocket money. The city didn't look like that place from the stories of those who came before me and it got me really sad, because from those stories I could see a place where I would have liked to live. The endless stories had no limits regarding politeness, helpfulness, and a proud feeling for being courteous towards others to make a cohesive and positive society.

Of course, those stories where idealized to some degree, but it's possible to analyze the data from past years, criminality rates, newspaper articles, etc. to see that huge changes had occurred in that city. I had the chance to confirm this theory a few years later. I was 22 by then and after visiting my first girlfriend in her Baltic country I thought it was a good idea to connect that trip with a second stay in London for a couple of months to do some more temp jobs before going on with my studies. The city I found in 2005 was visibly much worse than before. Everything was a bit messier and dirtier. It was harder to spot all-time Londoners as well. There was a lack of jobs everywhere, because of the massive amounts of people who had moved into the city from countries that no longer required a visa to travel there. It was the same thing I was doing, of course, going there to look for a job... good for them, and bad for me due to the high competition.

This time I went everywhere myself, I knew where all the agencies were, I had more education, more experience, all the documents available and ready from my previous trip, etc. I had done everything correctly and by myself. I felt that I had matured and somehow the big city that was so scary at 17 was more manageable a few years later. However, following the main idea of this book, those efforts were met with no reward whatsoever. Being more prepared, more easily employable, speaking the language better, going around the city as if it were my own, and having no luck after going to more than 20 interviews and visiting more than a dozen temp agencies. Remember that on my first trip I had tried two agencies and got hired in both of them missing half of the things people were saying to me. The fact that after all my improvements the results had been so devastatingly negative made me leave London thinking that the whole situation didn't make any sense at all, whatsoever.

It wasn't a story of personal growth that ends in a triumphant reward for your efforts and improvements... It was the exact opposite and it's one of the strangest feelings a human being can experience. Something like this:

Human: -Hey, I did everything I was supposed to. I overcame my limitations, I grew up as a person and all that. Where is my improvement on the results?
Life: -Hmm... What improvement?
Human: -You know... If before investing time and effort I was getting 30% of the results I wanted, now that I am doing things better I expect the results to be better as well.
Life: -Hmm... Nope.
Human: -Oh... Er... Ok... Well, can I still get my previous 30%?
Life: -Nah, changing circumstances outside your control. You get nothing
Human: -Oh well... I... I guess I'll just leave then...
Life: -Yes, go. Hurry up before I kill another one of your family

members with a cancer. How many do you have left? How is your last living relative doing these days?
Human: *runs out of the conversation screaming in panic*

If I told you now that my last direct relative underwent chemo recently you probably wouldn't believe me (she is fine now, but really... WTF life? This is insane!). I have no idea if my family had the habit of breaking cemetery tombstones before I was born, or if we were cursed by witches, or angered the old gods or the new ones in any way... But I can honestly tell you that one of these days I thought of going in a tour of temples: churches, synagogues, mosques, Buddhist places, Shinto altars, statues of Thor, etc. Apologizing or something, like: "Hi Buddha, hi Jesus, hi Horus, sorry for whatever I may or may not have done in this life or in previous ones. I apologize for whatever has caused this wrath from heavens to befall upon my family line in general and me personally... Can you stop killing everyone for some years? I took the liberty of calculating the odds of all this happening to the same person at this rate and if the probabilities of losing your dad before your teenage years were less than 1% in my school, the combined probabilities of losing your mom 10 years later, before you even turned 23 are astronomically low, but having to see cancer in your last direct relative a few years later was the moment when I lost my shit... Who's pulling the strings? What is this nonsense? All these difficulties and tragedies escape by far the softest statistical scrutiny. Life expectancy in my country is beyond 80 years old! Am I the next one? Have you come for me cold finger of death?? *looks around paranoid*"

And of course, this has affected me in very weird and twisted ways. Being alone seems even safe at this point. You struggle with your dark illogical thoughts and come to the conclusion that maybe for me it's better not to have children. This life doesn't seem to be the right type of place to invite more humans at this point. If something happened to me they would probably end up in an orphanage at this rate of untimely deaths and illnesses. The more I look at life, the more I see this as some sort of prison planet where nobody else should end up. But don't let me drag

you down with my views and opinions on this particular
subject... As you probably understand by now, I have no idea if
having children is right or wrong in absolute terms. It's just that
my personal circumstances make me inclined to see this planet
as mostly negative place with the occasional love story, beautiful
sunset, or afternoon fun at the beach with friends, but those
glimmering lights of joy and happiness still don't compensate for
all the suffering we get to experience as humans.

As I wrote before, this isn't a subject in which I would have any
interest for people to follow my steps. You could very well argue
that according to some Buddhist schools this planet and this life
is the perfect ground to test our humanity and our potential for
spiritual development and blah, blah... Without challenges to
face, how could we grow? The fact that some of those challenges
appear to be artificial or manufactured by external powers
beyond our control that defy basic statistics should be an
indication that Earth, as a planet (sorry for my lack of inclusivity
if you are reading this paragraph in the year 2086 from Mars or
so) is designed to provide us with circumstances that can make
us better beings. Yes, that theory would make some sense, for
sure...

But you would need to accept that there is some inherent or
intrinsic value in those tragedies and that only through those
dark episodes we could grow. I entirely disagree. I acquired some
of the individualistic parts of my character when I was a child
without anyone dying after a long illness. I would have developed
exactly the same in London with or without anyone missing from
the picture. A job offer in another continent would have the same
effect than those deaths... You would be alone and forced to rely
only on yourself. Not to mention that it creates this panic
towards the environment you are living in: "Err... can I try to
form a family of my own or will the children come with horrible
illnesses and my hypothetical wife would enter an alcoholic
depression and all that? Like... can I have a conventional and
statistically normal life with a house and a picket fence and oh...
the biggest economic crisis in decades, well ok then, I guess I will

get by and do my best and finish my doctorate and in a few years the situation will be back inside statistical levels of... Wait... a super-virus??? Really??? Who is directing this movie??? This is insane!!! The biggest financial crisis in living memory has barely finished 4 years ago and instead of peace and quiet for some decades we get a super-virus right away? Is this reality???"

I have no idea if bringing children into the world is ethically responsible at this point. It is not up to me to tell you if based on your circumstances, your possibilities, and the conclusions you got on the ethical aspect of the subject it is right for you to have children, but I kinda went from doubtful caution to an adamant refusal for myself. I keep wondering what will be the next bizarre episode in this weird story humanity is living. I don't want to write "super-volcano eruption" because if I happened to get it right I would feel like a prophet of doom. What I can tell you is that the type of person who CHOOSES to have children alone didn't clearly understand the implications of that decision, nor the ethical consequences of willfully saying: "I want to have a baby, I don't care if he/she suffers from not having a father/mother... The lordddd will provide for them". It's so deeply irresponsible and so incredibly selfish to bring another human being to this crazy world making them lack one of the two main figures in their lives, that I honestly doubt it can go unpunished at a spiritual level. And yeah, a few lines ago I wrote "father/mother" because I am not focusing only on those deranged women who want to be mothers without having established a suitable home with a stable partner first. I am also thinking about those men who pay some woman to carry their child and then disappear from the picture. Consciously forcing a child to grow without one of the two basic elements they require for even having a decent chance at a statistically normal life is insanely wrong.

So from my previous argument you can tell that I am quite ok with adoptions by single parents, gay parents, lesbians, polyamorous families, and any other social arrangement where the child goes from an impersonal orphanage to a decent house with love and care. I mean, we all have our limitations as humans and there are mechanisms in place to make sure the child is cared for and all that. Any house would be an improvement from an orphanage if there is love and care, but choosing to produce new humans without providing them the basic minimum requirements for a statistically regular life just because someone wants to be a mommy or a daddy is so wrong for so many different reasons, that I would need a separate book to list them all.

Anyhow, let me stop wagging my finger for a while and tell you about how my stock investments went after London. I went to the bank to open an account and got an investment one as well. I can safely say that in my life I have been more years investing than without investing cause I am 37 now and... well you do the math. I started awfully wrong, kept on losing a bit more, recovered something, then gained quickly, and then lost again... It was a rollercoaster of emotions in which I ended up with 20% less money than what I started with. I stopped investing for a while and then came back again to it a few years later winning fast, winning fast again, then getting a big chunk of my money buried in a company where the fundamentals were good, the board was smart, the results from the past 30 years had been consistent, but it was in a sector particularly affected by the crisis of 2008. After that every investment has produced benefits because I don't take chances. I invest when I see it perfectly clear, I get my 5 or 10 percent and I am out. I know investing experts will tell me that it's good to wait if there is potential for growth, and it's true in some markets and environments, but in my case I take nibbles of free money and I am content with that.

The stock market is a good place to put your ego in balance. You get rewarded for the theories and ideas that were right, and you get punished for blind greed and for being stubborn in your beliefs. Flexibility and humility are two things that the markets teach you without much effort, even if it takes you years to learn the lesson like in my case. I invest carefully now, without big expectations, and I am fully aware that I am out of my depth being a private and small investor with limited funds. I take my small gains, I say "thank you" and I look for the next clear opportunity. I know I am limiting myself, and it's for sure that I will never double or triple my capital, but as the money I invest grows, so does that 5% or 10% that I get from the operations. Once again this particular aspect of my life is not a story of awesome success, but a triumph of reason and common sense over ego. Knowing my limitations has helped me avoid making mistakes in this and other areas. For example I don't drive. I can't. I am an absent-minded person who doesn't remember the names of streets in his own city. Spatial awareness is not my strong suit, nor being focused on the road. It has always been clear to me that I would be a shitty driver and would potentially end up injuring myself or others. There is no shame in admitting it, and in fact I am a bit proud of this ability to understand my own personal limitations. There are things I do very well, and there are other things I am awful at, like focusing on menial repetitive tasks, silencing my inner thoughts, reading maps, remembering routes and visual points of reference, etc. Most of those things one needs for driving, so it is an exercise of responsibility to say: "Hey, I know our society functions with cars, I know they are good to get around, I know I would benefit from having one, but the risks for myself and others would be a price too big in exchange for those benefits".

Personal limitations also make me judge my shortcomings and those of others differently. I tend to value circumstances and specifics in a way in which if I see I am dealing with one of my strong points I will demand more from myself than from others. Likewise I am very lenient with my own weaknesses, even while proactively trying to improve them. For example I was watching a video about the founder of Domino's Pizza. His dad also died, his mom left him in an orphanage with his brother, he had to wash floors and stuff, then he ended up sleeping in a cold farm where he was working for very little money, before that his mom picked them up and abandoned them again, his brother left his pizza business, he got bankrupt before finally being successful, etc. I mean, yes there are lives that are as hard, or even harder than our own, but that guy became a billionaire so if we use his example as a reason to feel better about our own lives we should also ask: "hey... where are my millions?" I remember the stories of the African people I was working with. As I mentioned before some of them were from Cameroon, there was one guy from Congo, a girl from Mali, etc. they would tell you about the improvements they had had since moving to London, but they would also mention the lack of family ties, the difficulties of making friends, the absence of free land to run around or do whatever you wanted. You were not supposed to jump to the River Thames for a swim and stuff like that. In some parks they wouldn't even let you step on the grass or feed the duckies, which were unthinkable things in their countries. So yes, the money and the living conditions were better for them, but they started missing and giving value to things they used to take for granted when they were in their beautiful African lands.

Life is not the Olympic Games of tragedy and drama. It would be strange if when a pet dies someone said: "cheer up! It could have been worse! It could have been your parents!" Some people out there certainly have it more difficult than us, but when you deviate from the statistics is when you become an anomaly and you start feeling the lack of harmony and universal fairness with your particular situation. I remember my grandparents talking about playing barefoot on the streets with some ball made of cloth and glued pieces of leather. They were comparing that situation in regard to my brand new ball telling me how lucky I was and I didn't know why they were wrong back then, so I couldn't answer anything back, but I guess I know a bit more now and I can clarify my point of view. You just explained to a kid that lives in a high building surrounded by long streets with cars that during your childhood you had plenty of friends your age to play with; that it was as easy as wrapping a few cloths together and everyone would have fun the whole afternoon. They were all playing with the same rules, in the same conditions, and not having shoes or a real ball to play didn't matter statistically speaking because that was the norm. In other words, I guess it would theoretically be possible to take a millionaire with 6 or 7 houses and a helicopter, surround him with billionaires and make him depressed about the fact that he can't still afford to get his own private jet and mega-yacht with matching crews. Every single day he would judge his own situation by that of those surrounding him, and to tell you the truth I don't really know if that's fair or not.

Should we judge our situation based on objective universal standards? "Hey, you can get drinkable water from your faucet! You don't have to go to any well, you lucky you!" Aha... running water... great... but perhaps humans need a bit more than that to be happy. Or perhaps we should judge our general performance and luck based on those of our peers? After all, isn't that what we do with academic writings? Like: "Hey! I wrote a paper about cognitive abilities in pedagogical environments requiring specific needs, I showed it to a bunch of grannies knitting in the park and they thought it was awesome!" Aha... yes, but perhaps you need to focus on your PEERS, in order to clarify the quality of your academic writing? Nice and knowledgeable as those grannies may have been. I guess the easiest answer would be to look for some balance between the two positions, as always... If there is a huge statistical deviation between my peers and I whoever those may be depending on the context, changing my peers may be a viable alternative, or perhaps we could keep our peers while being mindful that we are only looking at a small portion of a bigger reality that encompasses more cases and circumstances than the ones we are obsessing about. But then again, in tragic situations where you have a broad statistic pool to focus on, if you choose to ignore that to focus on other specific samples you would just be cheating yourself. Coming back to my example with the death of my dad as a child, yes on the one hand you could look around your school and realize you are a statistical anomaly lower than 1%. On the other hand you could go to the nearest orphanage in the region and be happy that you still have a roof over your head and your mom will be with you for a few more years, but wouldn't that be disingenuous and intellectually dishonest? The ultimate checkmate regarding that mentality of "everything is relative" "happiness is an opinion" etc. would be to include those 83 orphan children in the city together with the other children from all the other schools and realize that they wouldn't really balance each other out. Yes, congratulations, we found the one statistical place that could make you feel better about your situation, but if we include those in the general group of "children your age in this city" you would inevitably go back to becoming a statistical anomaly of less than 1%, but now instead of being the first, second, or third child who has it worst in your group, you are the 84th from the bottom. However now there are luckier kids to look at! Thousands of them! If before you felt melancholic about random birthday celebrations wait until you see that by including all the children in your city you have some of them who are loved more than you, who have better families, better houses, supportive siblings that will later on help them in life, in business, parents that will live until their 80s in relative good health... So I don't know if this is good or bad for my mood and for yours, but at least it's honest logical thinking. Whenever someone tells you that some people out there have it worse than you in some aspect to make you stop complaining, you can always remind them that statistically speaking they are right, but plenty more people have it better than you as well so what do we do with those? Do we ignore them? Yes, 1% of kids have also suffered as much as you or perhaps even more, but do we ignore the other 99%? How does that make any sense at all?

Call me crazy if you wish, but I like balance and truth even in my statistics for tragedy and complaints. Does complaining really achieve anything? I think yes. As long as it doesn't prevent you from improving, acting, achieving, being proactive (yes I also hate this word but I can't think of any synonym right now) what is wrong about recognizing that you have it harder than others? It helps you being fair to yourself. It would be a bad start if we can't even be merciful and compassionate about our own lives. It dehumanizes us from a personal level to a general one. So yes, learning, achieving, improving... those things are all positive and necessary but where is the fairness or the honesty in ignoring where we have it easier or more difficult than others? It makes for a fair and balanced assessment of the situation. Sometimes people react as if by complaining about some statistical unfairness we are one step away from curling into a corner to cry for the next couple of years when in reality it can be a healthy exercise in self-recognizing the playing field we have been assigned in this life. From there we can keep striving and moving forward knowing that the difficulties we face are not our sole responsibility for being unable, or dumb, or useless, but the result of external circumstances that we need to take into account in order to have the strength to cope with them. An example? Well: Claudia Marie lives in the middle of the Sahara Desert, Claudia Marie wants to be a swimmer and compete at an amateur level, perhaps even representing her country in some tournament... I am sorry Claudia Marie, but the nearest swimming pool is three days away from your house. Through no fault of your own you are gonna have it much harder than the average person to fulfill your dreams, and indeed you could also work in the afternoons after your school in order for you to save for moving closer to a place with a swimming pool, but oh you wouldn't like to leave your parents alone to cope with the farm by themselves, so yes you could build some sort of swimming pool with vinyl, polymers, and an iron structure that could hold it all together and blah, blah, and train near your house but at which point exactly would you be within your right to say: "Damn... I just want to swim, universe! Let me live! Are the other competitors faced with the same dilemmas? Are they also buying building materials and water filters to just practice their favorite sport? Or am I a statistical anomaly that should keep these difficulties in mind to not falter or despair when I compare my performance with theirs?" I mean, wouldn't we all agree that Claudia Marie's bronze medal would feel as much a triumph or an achievement as that of whoever takes the gold one without all those difficulties? It's not about clapping mindlessly recognizing her tragic difficulties, it's more about describing reality as it is in order to keep a balanced point of view about things. You couldn't get that gold medal with the cards you were dealt in the game of life Claudia Marie, but we are even more proud of you for the good results you got facing those overwhelming odds against you. It's all about intellectual justice at this point.

I would like to talk a bit more about studies before going to the next chapter. I was one of those children with very good intelligence scores in the class tests. I am not saying that those keep stable and unaltered in time, nor am I bragging because it would be stupid considering how little I have achieved in life if those tests meant something significant. I just want to direct your attention to the fact that a psychologist from the city council came to our school, measured the children in my class, determined that I scored high as a kite in different areas, and nothing whatsoever happened after that: "Hey! This kid is very smart! Anyway, gotta go... bye!" So as a child you don't know how the world works, but you have the naive intuition, the childish innocent presupposition that something HAS to happen when they find out that you have potential. Why assessing it if nothing is going to happen anyway? Why the tests? Why bothering the students? No child got kicked out for being too dumb, no child got sent to another school for being too smart. Nobody spoke with my parents about different options or anything like that. Wouldn't it make more sense that, as a society, we keep an eye on those children that can be useful due to their capabilities? Even if only out of purely selfish reasons it's clear we are wasting intellectual resources that will never transform into profitable businesses, companies that create value, patents that enrich a region, thinkers that will make our lives better with their ideas and inventions... I am not talking about money invested directly on those children, but more about arrangements to ensure that they meet their true potential. I was bored to death the first years in my school, and without challenges I had to invest very little effort to reach the required marks. I never saw any incentive to strive for more. I took my grades seriously for a while, but then realized that nobody really cared. I could do all my homework in an hour and get a score of 70% or I could do everything perfectly well in three hours and score 95%. I preferred to play Super Mario and watch cartoons to be honest. I am sure those things were also good and healthy to relax your mind and learn other abilities and stuff like that, I just regret to admit that I owned my first telescope when I was 28. I had never used one before. I have no idea if that loss of potential is relevant in my case, but in the great scheme of things I am sure we are wasting a lot of talent from countless other people without a real reason for it.

Furthermore, whenever I see one of those famous athletes, golf players, F-1 pilots, etc. that started when they were six or seven I begin to think that I have never touched a racing car even to this day. I held a golf club for the first time inside a shopping mall in my 20s, and I went to athletics in my teens for a couple of years... The same story: "You run fast, kid... anyway, the class is over. Gotta go! Bye!" There is always this feeling that something should happen when you demonstrate ability and potential... but it doesn't in most cases. I am not saying that winning a medal at some regional championship would have fundamentally changed society in any way, but I am sure that from a statistical point of view if you leave enough talents from enough people unexplored, sooner or later you would be hurting society and yourself. The genius electrician who recognizes the dangers a future leaking pipe would have on your business saving it from bankruptcy, the talented makeup artist that helps your daughter get noticed by the love of her life, the lab wizard who recognizes some anomaly with one of the parameters of your blood sample and saves you from a certain death in a couple of years... The examples are as many as hidden talents are left unexplored, and although there will always be average professionals performing regular-quality tasks, whenever we need the best of the best, the exceptional people, and those have not had the chance to shine and prove their worth, we as a society are the ones who suffer.

Now for a little secret. Studies get easier the more you advance in them. I struggled more with first and second year phonetics in my degree (I studied among other things Modern Languages... Linguistics so to speak) than with my master studies. Theoretically speaking I think it would be easier to finish two master degrees of two years each than a four year degree. In the degree you kinda have to absorb the words and thoughts of others, which may prove difficult if you have a creative mindset, but in specialized diplomas and postgraduates you are supposed to create your own ideas and all that, so they will be worried about plagiarism and stuff like that, when in reality... for a creative person it's easier to express his own ideas rather than trying to paraphrase what someone else said two centuries ago. "Societies should function under clear premises and an effort on efficient results that benefit everyone" -Oh I see that you have been reading Jean Jacques Rousseau lately! Haven't you? "Err... not really, it just makes sense that societies operate like that without some philosopher from centuries ago having to tell us these things". So, I guess what I am saying is that postgraduates get really easy as you grow older because you start having opinions about everything and you welcome with passionate fruition the slightest opportunity to write them down anywhere. So regardless of your age and circumstances there is no point in getting obsessed about high school when you can fix anything with a degree, and there is no point in making the degree the new obsession when you can fix everything with a postgraduate or two, and above all a PhD from a humble university will always be higher than a graduate from the most prestigious institution. I am not encouraging you to aimlessly study for years without a goal or professional purpose. I think I have already mentioned that my doctorate has not turned me into any of my childhood idols. I am just pointing out the fact that there are usually many ways to reach our goals, even if after achieving those goals we realize that we have been achieving for nothing (get it? The title of the book... heh... ok next chapter).

CHAPTER THREE: Policeman, no... Diplomat, no... Military Officer!

I had always had the dream of being a cop. The ideal of protecting society from dangers and people who lost their way momentarily or found it in hurting others deliberately. I had an idealized version of cops that I will always refuse to give up. I have lived in several countries and I have experienced everything from pure admiration to a disdainful condemnation depending on the situation. The cops in Spain were mostly as idealistic as myself. Even when you think the job has grinded them down and broken their spirits, you see them proving you wrong by doing something heroic and altruistic. In UK they gave me the impression of being a bit less committed to the citizens than to maintaining their jobs... an opinion that is purely personal and very limited considering I only lived in London and for a limited amount of time. The cops in Sweden and Denmark gave this friendly vibe that was really refreshing. When you approach one a smile usually appears on their faces. I have no idea if it's a trained feature or a genuine one but there is some primal reaction towards that attitude: "Oh! This person is happy to see me! I just made a friend! This interaction will surely be positive!" In Poland they looked a bit more serious but were overtly welcoming when they saw you were a foreigner in need of assistance. In Ireland the Garda were just as kind and charming as your average Irish person, but with a particularly helpful disposition. In Serbia it was a disgrace to see a cop half-drunk with his weapon almost falling out of his holster in the public transport. The girl I was dating at the time explained me that he was having an affair with a married woman and for some reason the whole scene seemed grotesque to me. The beautiful policewomen at the Nicola Tesla airport were certainly much more professional than that guy, but statistics won't be any good in this case... I would be unable to say if they chose those three spectacular girls for that particular assignment specifically to give a positive image to the travelers, or if it was just a random coincidence since the average Serbian girl in a police uniform would look just as spectacular for a tired traveler. I have encountered more cops in other countries but I don't want to bore you too much with this subject. My main point with this is that there are many ways to perform the job, from counter-terrorist sniper to customs officer, homicide detective, or kind patrolman who smiles politely to a lost tourist in need of help. I always liked the ideals of the job, so I tend to respect the uniform a lot.

I couldn't become one because of the need for a driving license. When I was at the driving school I realized I wasn't cut out for that. After the car license you need to get one for motorbikes and another one for driving vehicles with sirens, even before applying to join the police academy. My desires for being a cop crashed against the harsh realities of my awful driving skills. I had also considered diplomacy so I went to an introductory course for that type of stuff at the place where those guys get selected and trained. It wasn't at all how I expected it to be, although this could perfectly be blamed on the system in place in my particular country of birth. They explained us the process step by step and to summarize it in a nutshell, 20 years moving around awful destinations as a third or second level secretary. The surnames of the diplomatic staff in my country repeat suspiciously and they calculate that 6 or 7 families control the entry exams, performance reports, destination assignments, etc. so entering from the outside world and becoming an ambassador in some place would be near impossible. But as always, there are other ways and alternatives to explore.

If you get enough political influence or you manage to position yourself well enough within a party, you can be named ambassador right there and then. This habit is more common in small countries where there isn't a centralized diplomatic school to educate their Foreign Service members. It's also common in countries like the U.S. where being appointed to represent the country is really usual. If you have money and some office or suitable residence you could request being appointed as Honorary Consul for some foreign country. You are supposed to have ties with the country you are going to represent, and be ready to pay the expenses of giving service to the citizens of that country, so this gives you mostly troubles unless you use the powers of this position in shady specific ways. Depending on the autonomy the foreign country has granted you, you could make your residence have diplomatic immunity. You could also decide who gets a passport or an appointment at your consulate, so technically speaking you could open a few doors that are highly unusual for regular people. It could also be the base for business deals, and it's always interesting to have diplomatic options to play games of influence with them if that's your thing.

Last but not least you could also get a position as a cultural or military attaché to some embassy. The cultural one seems to be the easiest one to achieve, and I guess that if you make enough noise and the embassy ends up needing you, you could leverage yourself into that position. If you are a university teacher organizing cultural activities related to your language and culture, people will start wondering why are you doing more for the image of your country than the embassy, and from that situation you can collaborate with them in exchange for being named the official representative of anything cultural that has to do with your country or language in some other country.

I am not sure if this information is interesting for everyone in general or if it has limited impact but those types of strange relatively unknown ways have always fascinated me. There is always some caveat, some bureaucratic door to go through, some different way of doing things, and that also includes the Armed Forces.

So after deciding I should postpone my diplomatic interests until I can directly be appointed ambassador or I can afford to have my own consulate, I directed my attention to the Armed Forces. I figured that if I couldn't be a policeman I could become a military officer which is also quite interesting and cool. I didn't want to study four more years for that, so I checked the option of entering the equivalent of the National Guard for the U.S. or the Territorial Army in U.K. but in my country. After a hard selection process with too many candidates for every position I was fortunate enough to enter the Air Force as a pedagogical officer. My duties would be related to linguistics, teaching courses of different subjects, translations, and stuff like that.

First they train you as a soldier for a short period of time, and then they train you as an officer also with a crash course on everything you need to know. After that you are supposed to go through two more training periods that I didn't even manage to complete... You see, after all the paperwork, the selection process, the requirements, getting the appointment, and entering the Air Force... the budget of the program got obliterated due to the economic crisis and its aftermath. In the nine years that I have been in that program they didn't even let me finish the two mandatory trainings I had left. This must be quite shocking for anyone who has an idea of how a military institution should function, but it will shock you even more to know that my country is a NATO member. So this was another one of those situations where you put effort into something, you work hard to achieve your goal, you succeed, and then absolutely nothing relevant happens. At all. It's an increasingly frustrating feeling to see that you keep achieving the things you wanted but then they get blurred and disappear into an abyss of irrelevance. I got to enter, got trained, wore the uniform a few times, then waited for nine years when nothing happened, then I was out... That was all my military experience, and it's a bit embarrassing when someone asks me and I have to tell them that technically I have "served" in the armed forces as an officer for 9 years, and didn't set foot on a military base after my training. It's really sad to talk with reserve officers from other countries and realize that once again you are a statistical anomaly and even in more humble nations they manage to run their armed forces with a bit more logic.

Surprisingly I have started observing this phenomenon in other countries and environments. True that mostly in dysfunctional ones (the environments, I mean). Take for example the Oscars. It must be quite frustrating to get one of those statues for best actor or actress and then not make any more movies. I have no idea why it happens but it seems to be so for a lot of them. They get the statue, they give a short speech, they thank some people, they cry tears of happiness, and then they don't get selected for any more roles. That's precisely the feeling one gets in some circumstances. It would be one thing to not achieve some goal... you would learn from it, become humble, and all that. But if you achieve your dreams and goals and they end up being meaningless there is a certain void of illogical chaos that is hard to fill. When that happens a few times you start wondering if there is any point in anything: "Congratulations! You got your black belt! There are no battles or monsters to fight so... nothing happens! Oh! Congratulations again! You got your PhD! There are no positions for you, the crisis and all that... you know... Nothing happens, sorry kid! Oh! Congratulations again! You became an officer! Oh my! You are on fire! Unfortunately nothing will happen in the next 9 years, sorry kid... Oh! You decided to study another specialty? Two even??? Well... let's see if now something will *laughing in the background* nah, sorry... nothing happens once again!"

This phenomenon is entirely endemic of our current times. When you speak with people from older generations they ALL agree that there was some correlation between efforts invested and results obtained. You can check documentaries and biographies about the French Revolution, the American Civil War, WW1, WW2, the economy of the 50s, 60s, 70s... You can even reach the 80s and early 90s with some movies where the guy doesn't have any education or experience but he is willing to learn and he enters the business and he grows little by little thanks to his passion and blah, blah... That doesn't happen nowadays. None of it. We are the generations that are achieving for nothing.

We go into a world where the figures of authority and wisdom that already got some experience in life look at the younger generations and realize they are all in the same boat. I had students asking me if completing a postgraduate will increase their chances in some professional career. I have no idea what to answer. I had young kids asking me how I managed to become an officer and how they could do it themselves. I have to look at them and admit that it's all a façade... They see an adult that has achieved things they want to achieve and they assume you have it all figured out... I don't. I am as clueless as they are during this particular time in history we are living in. So instead of being this beacon of light that can show them the way, I have to sit down with them and explain them that currently most of us keep achieving things and improving ourselves but that doesn't translate into meaningful results.

My parents studied far less than me, they spoke less languages, they lived in less countries, they read less books about investing, and yet they managed to acquire a house with relative ease, they got jobs where good performance was rewarded with personal growth, and they put their savings in shares of their local bank, that got bigger and wealthier like all the other companies in the 70s. Their limited efforts gave relatively good results. And you may think it was something personal or circumstantial, but I can easily dispel that notion right away. I managed to still experience some of the good times, and to see it all fall apart. In the 70s and early 80s they had two perfumeries that were allowing them to live like upper-middle-class. They started opening the first shopping malls in my city and suddenly they had to close one of the two commercial spaces they had. There wasn't enough money to be made. In the 90s they opened yet another shopping mall, the beginning of the 2000s saw the rise of internet, and suddenly the same mentality, behavior, and attitudes that had provided comfortable living results for a big part of the population were not enough to even keep a small business open. "Oh, renovating your attitudes is the key! They should have gone to those shopping malls and establish there a...." Yeah, yeah, I saw family friends who went down that road and ended up closing down their shops even faster. I am telling you, the people who had been resourceful and entrepreneurial in the 70s and 80s didn't become retarded in the next decade and a half... It's the world that began to change rapidly and without control. Things have only gone downwards from there and we have reached a point where some people have started referring to the situation as a "gig economy". And if you still think this is pure pessimism and the model can't be applied to other areas, let me hammer down the point getting away from small businesses to focus on prestigious professions from the past. In the 50s and

60s if you were a lawyer you were supposed to have a
comfortable financial situation. Nowadays getting a law degree
and being good at what you do is no guarantee of any
professional success. You can see how most professions have
fallen from those pedestals of social respect and correlation
between effort invested and results obtained. Not convinced yet?
Flight attendants... Tell me that profession hasn't changed for
the worse in the last decades. Even airline pilots have seen their
conditions and salaries reduced. The competition is fierce and
the automated flying systems are a few steps away from making
that profession even more difficult.

New professions perhaps? Well I was following a couple of
personal blogs from tech guys and it was fascinating to see them
earning cool salaries in their early 20s, but years later one of
those two is currently unemployed and the other one had to find
a job abroad and is earning less than when he started his
professional career. Let me make this clear again... My point is
not to invite you to wear an orange robe, pick up a drum and join
me in screaming "the end is nay!" on the streets. We are just
analyzing the social and economic developments that have made
things more difficult and less logical than in past decades. It's
that lack of logic that makes the playing field muddy and weird.
I have made more money working one month a few hours per day
than selling kilos (pounds, stones, Egyptian elbows, whatever
you use in your area) of silver. One would open the bag and see
all those rings, medals, bits of silver I wanted to get rid of and
think that it would be enough to buy a small castle... but nope,
all that silver would not even cover a month of my salary back
then and it was surprising somehow. You can buy original first
editions of famous books for a few dollars but a university
textbook printed in cheap paper or a vegan recipe book printed
this year would cost you more: "Uh! That guy has a first edition
of Mark Twain, he must be rich!" Hm... not really... 45 bucks for
owning a piece of literary history. Somehow too many things
don't make a lot of sense and that takes away our reference
points, I think.

So, with all these examples that can be easily verified through statistical analysis I am trying to convey the message that even though the world has gone through hard times before, things made sense and there was some order and common sense in it all. Yes, the Second World War was awful and all that, but if you were a mathematical genius you would eventually end up in cryptographic stuff, if you spoke German you would end up in espionage or communications, if you were in good shape and could shoot well you would end up in a sniper company, and if you have imagination and can come up with effective ideas you would end up deceiving the Germans in some counter-intelligence division... Things made sense... The bombs fell, it was awful, but society made sense and it was logical. It could be that everything made sense because there was an imminent danger, so instead of nepotism, ideological like-mindedness, or random mechanisms, you wanted the best people to occupy the right positions for them because it was vital to win the war, to reconstruct the country, to face new challenges... As soon as those threats and dangers disappeared, the collective well-being was abandoned in favor of personal gain, so even though some people from the older generations were still around, you began to see the new generations acting up and signifying themselves by wearing weird clothes, doing weird stuff, and opposing "the establishment"... The same establishment that had won a war a couple of decades ago now saw these ungrateful newcomers screaming about anything they could. Fast forward two or three decades and the irredeemable grunge idols of yesterday are the ones that value the achievements of their country, the traditions, the history, and the society they used to hate so much.

In case you are a billionaire mastermind now or at some point in your life, I am not suggesting that a state of perpetual crisis and existential emergency is the best to put everyone in their rightful place for human development or anything like that. At some point we need to come up with the right self-sustainable structures that guarantee efficiency because of the control mechanisms in place for it, and not only because of a momentary need for survival destined to fade away after every crisis. Like:

-Hey, what happened to that Turing guy that broke the enigma code? Was he set for life after the war with a huge state pension?
-Oh, you don't wanna know...
-What happened to Churchill? He surely won the reelection after winning the war!
-Err... nope... he lost.
-What about the special operations guys? Those risked a lot... Were they recognized and...
-Well, not really... One of them became a popular actor... He played Dracula. Cool guy.

So it's not sustainable to keep resorting to exceptional circumstances to make things work as they should. Systems of checks and balances would be more effective into instilling this habit in the population. The idea that efficiency is good for everyone and to achieve top results we need to have everyone where they need to be is something that will (or should) probably be reinforced through artificial intelligence. Identifying talents, looking for them, recruiting them, etc. would be easier with vast computational power available. It would also be useful for us as functioning members of a society in the way that some of the best books, songs, shows, or videos we discover sometimes are totally unknown for other people. That wonderful knowledge, the enjoyment, the experiences... Perhaps they would be easier to access with artificial intelligence helping the process.

CHAPTER FOUR: Trips, Love, and Friendship in my life

My trip to London had been my first flight. Before that I had only been a passenger in cars, trains, and buses. After coming back to my country, besides investing a bit, I began working as a waiter, phone operator, electronics clerk at a shopping mall, and as an English teacher. Life had been quite dull between my studies and random jobs here and there. One thing we tend to forget is the existence of empty spaces in between periods. Those are kinda boring so we never tell about them and it ends up looking as if we go from one things to the next in a harmonious flow. It's rarely the case... especially with me. After London I spent two or three months unemployed and helping in the family business. I hated that place. I was supposed to sell things I wasn't using so it didn't matter how much I read the features and the information available about the makeup products, the lotions, the moisturizers, etc. The girls and women who entered the shop would stare at me every time letting me know that wasn't my place and they weren't comfortable talking about their skin issues with me. It would be difficult to count the times I received inappropriate comments about my knowledge, expertise, or openly derogatory statements that I had to let go most of the times because answering something cool usually meant scaring away a regular customer:

-Me: You need to consider that your skin tone has changed in summer after you tanned, but now that October is coming your skin will get lighter so it's better to choose one less tone than what you...
-Customer: Have you ever used the products from this brand? *giggles*
-Me: Err... no but they offer seminars about their products.
-Customer: I think I know a bit more about these things. I'll take the darkest one.

Customer service in a family business selling products for women being a young guy was one of the most exasperating scenarios one could imagine. I only saw a similar case to mine... The woman who sold me my first boxing gloves was a blonde lady in her late 50s. I remember being respectful and casual about the whole thing but hearing her talk about ounces, impact surfaces, and grips had mesmerized me. I remember most kids were always curious about the opportunities I had for picking up girls having so many of them entering the shop each day. I never in my life had any girl flirting with me in there unless they already knew me from some other place. Yet another one of those situations where it would be impossible to convince any scriptwriter that this is real life:

-Scriptwriter: So the girl enters the shop and she sees this kid her age, muscled from all the karate and what not, she approaches the counter and licks her upper lip in anticipation of...
-Me: Nope. Never. Not even once. I am not saying it wouldn't happen with one particular girl. I am saying that from all the girls that ever entered the shop not one would...
-Scriptwriter: Nonsense! It's the perfect setting for talking to a young guy with the excuse of...
-Me: I am not arguing about your reasoning... I am explaining you that the same witches that cursed my family with untimely deaths must have also put a curse on me or that place because I never experienced any attention helping there, alone or not.

Some of those situations defy common sense and go against everything a sane person would expect or imagine. Like when you see rock stars that abused drugs, alcohol, and lack of sleep live past their 70s, and any friend who tried to emulate them ended up like a broken toy in less than a decade.

Anyhow, I just wanted to make that reminder about the empty spaces in between episodes where something happens, because otherwise it would seem as if everything is occurring in a tight timeline full of action and stuff. There's a lot of gaming and writing in my notebooks while wondering what is wrong with me exactly. I mentioned the notebooks a couple of times by now and they would be the equivalent of a diary for future projects or something like that. I guess that's the best way to describe them. Let's say that I am 19 and I wonder what would take to create my own martial arts system. I would start writing different combinations, eliminating weaker options, review my specialized books and magazines for a few hours. Write down some of the weirdest combinations and end up calculating how much money and time it would take me to acquire all those skills, to register the federation, to design the program for the students... I would look for commercial spaces for rent in different cities, add those calculations, and increase those 20% for unexpected repairs or insurance fees... And then I would smile, look around me, and realize I have wasted a perfectly good evening doing something without any semblance of practical use. That wasn't even the weirdest one. After I came back to my country from UK I started to like a girl, a friend of a friend. She was really sweet and cool before I had gone away, but in these two years she had started smoking, dating some guy, breaking up with him, some more smoking, complaining about her ex... I still fancied her but instead of a 110% it would be an 85%. One day I started thinking: "what if I lost my virginity with her, but the condom broke and she got pregnant, and her family didn't want her to have an abortion and..." So I began collecting supermarket and shopping mall brochures, trying to guess how much it would cost me to raise a child and establish a family, which things I could use from when we were babies, how much wood I would need to build a cradle, how high would my salary have to be to take care of the hypothetical family, how much would I spend buying shirts, etc. I know it sounds totally insane and I wouldn't blame you for being skeptical about my weird habits, but I can honestly say I spent more than two days for sure with this hypothetical case that would never come to happen. So, if I was doing this amount of planning at 18 before even losing my virginity, you can imagine my reaction whenever I see a married couple not having a clue about those things. Lack of preparation goes against my deepest core beliefs.

A couple more years went by. I was 21 and I fell in love with a girl from the Baltic area that I met in a chatroom called ICQ (the chatrooms, not the chatting program... they had two and they were popular back then). I traveled to her country, this time alone and crossing the whole continent. She was totally different from the girls I had met so far, and there was some innocent light shining inside her that some people seem to have until they no longer do, and then you start wishing with all your heart that the same thing doesn't happen to you, and you try to convince yourself that maybe her light was never there because you are too afraid to think people could change so much and forget who they really are like that. *sad violin music plays*

I had no idea how "traveling" to such countries was supposed to go, and I was entirely by myself so, even though at 21 I should have known how things worked more or less, I felt myself quite unprepared for the experience. I was carrying a lot of wrong ideas that affected my abilities a lot. For starters I had been told at my bank that in such small countries they would be happy to accept euros when, in reality, they were quite proud of their small currency. I had a paper with 3 alternatives for accommodation and I figured I would have time to check one or two since I was arriving at 19:45. A taxi ride, a quick shower and to bed... I didn't count on the fact that there would be a delay of a couple of hours with my flight. I had no idea either that I would have to wait for my suitcase for half an hour more, and I quickly realized after 22:00 the currency exchange booths were closed. I started feeling anxious after realizing my phone's roaming wasn't active. I was unable to make or receive calls so this idea I had of casually picking my phone and calling the three hotels to see which one had available accommodation became less and less viable. I thought about phone booths but the ATM had only given me bills and there were no shops or bars to buy anything and get coins as change. The airport was deserted at that hour of the night and I had no idea why. I don't remember ever seeing such a thing in the other airports I visited after that trip. It's true that at 3:00 am most establishments inside an airport would be closed, but at 23:15 it seemed a bit unexpected.

Be it as it may, I got on a taxi and asked the man to take me to the nearest of the three hotels I had on my list. The driver spoke no English at all, and I was unable to tell him to wait in case the hotel had been full. It wasn't full! Such good luck, but the rude apathetic girl at the reception informed me that they only had double rooms available, the ones for honeymoons and stuff like that. I sighed and started filling the paperwork for the room, she grinned and told me that the price would be the equivalent of one week in a normal room. I stopped writing, grabbed my passport from the counter and left. I had almost been swindled, but oh! Not me, no sir, I was too smart for falling for the old trick of the double room that... I looked around me and realized I was alone late at night in a foreign country where I didn't speak the language and had no idea how to find a taxi. My phone's roaming still didn't work and fidgeting with the settings and options didn't seem to help. Despite years of martial arts I felt myself a bit vulnerable in that situation. At least now I had some coins from the change the taxi driver had given me. I went inside a phone booth and... it was only for electronic phone cards.

I looked around and saw a lady walking a dog. I figured she wouldn't be scared of me approaching her late at night, so I tried to use my English, my Spanish, and my limited French. It was useless. I showed with gestures that I needed a phone card to use the booth, but she didn't understand and she was kind enough to take me to her apartment to let me use her phone. That was the level of innocent hopelessness I must have projected that night. That lady's name was Olga Temaeva and that night she was like a guardian angel that saved me from sleeping in a public park. I called the girl I was there to meet and I explained her the situation. They talked in Russian for a bit (Russian is quite a common conversational language in this country I refuse to mention to try and protect my identity). Olga called a taxi for me, and she rejected the money I offered her with a gesture that made me realize I was risking offending her if I insisted. She waved me farewell with a smile and I left to the house of the girl I went to visit. For a guy who forgot his own birthday and doesn't remember the names of people who studied with him for years, you can imagine how impressed I was by that lady's behavior that day to remember her name even now. Moments like those inspire you to be a better person I think.

What happened after that was everything you could imagine from a former Soviet country in the year 2004 or 2005, I don't remember. The building looked like a place from some nightmare, the family was suspicious of the foreigner, but the girl was beautiful and happy to see me there, so everything was ok in the end I guess. Episodes like these made me realize that traveling with insufficient funds is an extreme sport. Only money can save you from certain unpleasant situations and allow you to keep some of your dignity, so I try to be prepared whenever I travel and I always go with the mentality that the universe is out to get me, and that I better prepare contingency plans for every single possible circumstance that could go wrong.

This was my first experience in a relationship, and also for her. We had met chatting online as I mentioned and we had liked each other very much. After my visit I came back home, then traveled there once more in winter. During that visit she took me to an ice ring but since it was my first time skating I was going very slowly. After a while the girl got a bit frustrated with my skills and she let go my hand to go at her usual speed for a few rounds. I felt the clumsiest person in the world trying not to fall. I fell down hard once and my eyebrow began to bleed a little. When I was getting up I saw everyone else jumping, teens doing cool tricks, couples going really fast... so I said to myself: "Come on, you can do this... Get up and try to do what you were told with your feet!" The second time I fell down it was even harder than the first one and I hit my mouth against the ice. I had no idea how exactly the whole thing happened but I saw half of my front tooth flying away and never got it back. I stood up as best as I could and I remember thinking that this girl was not the right one for me after all... She had let go my hand and I had fallen... I know the rationale behind it might sound too weak, but I chose to see that as a sign, which is weird for a logical person.

I had to go to a dentist to reconstruct my tooth and she did an awesome job. Dr. Marina Osipova was her name. Just as before, I want to reiterate that my memory is awful for names, so you can tell that this woman was the best damn dentist I had ever met in my life. Her skills were not of this world. My tooth looked even better than before when I left her office in a humble building with worn-out equipment. As you know by now, those situations really get on my nerves. That dentist should have been the Director of some international research center, or the Dean of Advanced Dentistry in the most renowned university of that part of the world, yet here she was... performing her magic skills on an idiot who thought he could skate just as well as everyone else on his first day at an ice ring.

Anyway, the girl came to my country in summer, and I decided to move there and try to find a job after that. It was one of the craziest decisions I ever made. I started in that small Baltic nation from the bottom with private classes, then a short stay at a high school, then assistant lecturer at a university, and an offer to teach at a second one, then the second academic year I was a normal lecturer. That meteoric rise could be summarized by the interactions with the mother of the girl:

Her: It's teachers' day, but you are not a real teacher... You just teach private lessons after all.
Her a bit later: That high school you got in is better than the one I work at... Interesting.
Her a bit bit later: Happy Teachers' Day! We are colleagues!
Me: Ap, pap, pap... I teach at a university... I am an academic. We are not colleagues.

I know it sounds awful, and I really don't feel that way at all, honestly. A teacher is a teacher regardless of where he or she imparts knowledge. However under those circumstances it felt good to use that moment to prove myself that I had progressed and grown a bit since I first arrived to that country. I didn't like the family of the girl very much, but I was in love and my mom had recently died so the professional success I was having in the Baltics and having a hot beautiful girlfriend were the two things that kinda balanced the universe for me at the time.

I can honestly tell you thanks to the privacy of my identity, that I never had anything with one of my students. A few of them flirted here and there every once in a while, but I was proud to be loyal, although I did fantasize a few times with the possibilities that were being offered to me because... well, I am a human being. I felt like saying "Thank youuuu!" every time a girl or a colleague flirted with me. Years of being ignored working at a perfumery had left me thinking that perhaps I wasn't worthy of interest, so I felt vindicated with the way things were going now. I saved a bit of money and I bought a property: a garage for motorboats near the center of the city. I cleaned it, had big plans for it, but there was a dog at the entrance of the cooperative of garages that would bark menacingly at me every time I went to visit my garage. I had no idea why... everyone else seemed to enter without the slightest problem, and other dogs were always friendly with me. After arguing in my limited Russian a few times with the guy at the entrance, and even taking my knife out in one of the occasions when the dog ran directly at me ready to bite, I realized that situation wasn't worth the trouble. The oak bears the snow until it breaks, but the young pine tree bends, lets the snow fall, and then goes back to his original position unburdened. Beautiful, right? An old Buddhist saying... Well a few years later that cooperative got sold to build huge buildings and shops. God knows how much money each one of those garages was worth in that operation and mine was a double unit. No injustice there, just a usual casual complaint about my bad timing, but the responsibility was entirely mine this time. I wanted to study an MA in my country and I thought it would be strange to keep a garage in a place I wasn't sure I would go back to.

I was living with this girl in my country and I remember it as one of the happiest periods of my life. The weather was nice, the university was cool, I could train Thai Boxing and Brazilian Jujutsu in the mornings, make love before lunch, go to my classes, and come back for dinner, movies, laughter. We had the beach a few steps away from our building so that was awesome too. It's interesting how the same people could be happier with a better surrounding. I think we had everything we needed back then, but living in another city without work and burning savings wasn't a sustainable situation, so we had to go back to my city which although far from being a paradise, wasn't half bad either.

We started talking about having children and I explained my position about this world not being suitable for my hypothetical offspring, and all that. After a few conversations I realized this girl didn't see me as a goal, but rather as a means to an end, with the goal being "completing a puzzle". The puzzle would consist on a long relationship, a bit of fun, and then babies and an established family. Nothing wrong with wanting those things actually, but it suddenly dawns on you that you are not the center of somebody's universe... You are just an intermediate step to reach the final goal for some girls THAT happens to be motherhood. I remembering covering all the basic questions in subsequent conversations to realize if I was being truly loved for myself or not. The answers didn't disappoint: "A mother will always love her children more than her husband", "If you couldn't get me pregnant and the treatments didn't work I would have to find another partner", "I don't want to adopt someone else's children, I want my own", etc.

Then something strange happened. I got a summer position at the University of Copenhagen at the same time that she got a job there too for which she didn't meet the necessary requirements. I used my dark arts to make all the lies she had included in her CV more plausible and difficult to check, and we both went to Copenhagen after a short stay in Sweden. I had been chatting with an amazing girl from the Balkans after finding out that I was in a relationship where I was seen as little more than a prospective sperm donor that would need to accept that children take first place for "the puzzle girls". I thought it was the right time to end the relationship and start something new with this Balkan girl that had only been a platonic thing at the distance, but before throwing away a relationship of several years I decided it would be wise to test if my thoughts were true.

I created a fake profile in a website she was using for languages, I put on a few nice pictures from an amateur male model from France, and I began to chat with my girlfriend validating all her ideas: "But of course this life is about having children! What else is there to do? Being a mother is the most important thing in the world! Love should always take a step back or even die to let way for a loving family... The children are our future!!!"

She began to be more distant with the real me, and to send me more and more messages where she finally agreed that her boyfriend wanted different things, that she thought about breaking up with him, that now that there was this new door opening in her life everything was different and she could finally "be brave" to care about her own needs and blah, blah... The usual jargon for which someone should come up with a translation app of some sort:

Basic Girl: "I should be brave to love... I must follow my heart... Perhaps it's the time to allow myself to be happier with a new love and build something meaningful together".
Translation: "I should silence my conscience telling me I am cold and selfish... I should do what I please... Perhaps now that I found a new guy I should dump the old one and fulfill my ultimate goal in life, which is getting pregnant a couple of times".

With the fake profile I told her it was finally time to meet in person and she agreed she would break up with the real me if she liked the other guy more. I didn't go to that date to expose her or anything like that... I ghosted her, and then wrote a message saying it had been fun to check how unethical some girls could be, leaving their loving boyfriends for strangers who tell them a couple nice things and blah, blah... She called me that same day to ask how my day was going, to tell me she missed me, to tell me perhaps she had been a bit distant lately because of her job and other issues... I had to break up with this girl and fast.

I know some people might think that what I did was crazy wrong. The way I see it, it's a dangerous gamble. If you are wrong in your suspicions you become a paranoid psycho who goes around testing innocent people for crimes they would never commit, so to speak. But oh... if you happen to be right... You feel like an astute mastermind that can end a relationship clean as a whistle and without any emotional baggage or "what ifs". It feels liberating and righteous to end it all with good reasons, after being betrayed, and a bit before the other person was about to leave you. As I said, a dangerous ethical gamble... Fail and you become a toxic partner with trust issues. Be right and you become an innocent victim who was sensible enough to protect his heart and future from the forces of darkness.

Anyhow, after Denmark I went to the Balkans, of course. The girl was so beautiful and amazing. Living with her was awesome. She loved to play video games, she cooked an amazing pizza. She had never been in a relationship before so everything was new and wonderful for both of us. She told me one day that it was the first time in her life that she had felt truly happy, and I felt proud of myself for some reason. As if I was the sole cause for that happiness... "Behold! The Joy-Bringer!" It was cute and interesting to reinvent myself like that in such a short period of time. The Balkans weren't for me, at least at that time though. It's never a good sign when someone gets shocked after you give them back their money cause they provided you with the wrong change. The three times it happened when I was there were clear indications that perhaps that area of the world and I were walking different paths... The first time my girlfriend had to explain to the supermarket lady that there wasn't anything wrong with the bill, that I didn't want another one, that she had simply given me more money than she should. It took well over three minutes to make this lady understand that for the first time in her life a customer was handing her back money that wasn't his to keep. I became a legend at that supermarket, and that's a bit sad. The second time it happened the guy looked at me as if he had seen an alien; as if I didn't know money could be exchanged for goods and services even when someone hands you the wrong change. The third time was epic... I had to argue for a while with my girl so that she went back to the guy who sold the tickets in the bus to the capital, so she could hand him the extra cash that wasn't ours. An old lady shouted something at her and became emotional. My girlfriend came back and my face of pure shock, turned into a proud smile: The lady had told her that she was happy there were still young decent people in that country. I felt it unnecessary to rub salt in the wound. That old lady was really sweet.

Something strange happened to that Balkan girl in the space of a few months. She began to say that video games were a waste of time, that eating pizza regularly was not good, that she was too young to be living with a boyfriend, that she was in a very serious relationship and that she preferred to feel free and unbound by the ties of commitment, etc. I don't have all the pieces of this story, but either she started getting attention from other guys at her university, or she genuinely had an honest epiphany about video games and pizza not being her cup of tea anymore. Be it as it may, I went back to my country, she visited me there for the summer, and then we broke up, then she wanted to get back together and asked me to ignore her silly moods whenever she said she wanted to break up, and then she broke up again, this time for good. I don't have any negative feelings towards her I think... There isn't any poetic justice, she doesn't come back begging a few months later or anything like that... Just a sweet fun girl who started changing all the cool fun parts about herself due to internal or external pressure... I dunno about that girl, but video games and pizza never stopped being awesome for me so... she can enjoy whatever she is eating and doing in her free time these days. I never knew anything about her after that.

After the Balkans, again to my country. This was the time when I became an officer and also began teaching at a university. I had some Benjamin Button thing going on with my dating life because after a long relationship came a shorter one, and now I was happy to just date casually and visit or being visited by girls for a couple of weeks and back to their countries: "Oh... I wish our countries weren't so far away..." "Yeah, me too, but you can come next summer if I am not dating anyo... I mean if the circumstances allow". This would probably make the delights of any psychotherapist, but I don't think it was something deep or meaningful related to the pain of breakups or the fear of getting hurt again or any of that nonsense. It was fun and cool to be with beautiful girls even if it could only be for a limited period of time. Someone comes to your touristic country, she sees your profile, contacts you, and tells you after the summer she has to go back to wherever she came from to go on with her studies and try to fix things with her ex and what not... So you are posed with a choice now: do you enjoy this girl's company for a couple of weeks knowing there won't be any relationship after that, or do you tell her you are not interested in her perfectly-shaped body, and her divine face because you are looking for true love?

It would be like saying you prefer being homeless because your dream home is a palace, or claiming you will be unemployed until you can finally have the job of your dreams. In my humble opinion one can have high aspirations and at the same time enjoy the choices and opportunities available until those aspirations can be realized. The problem? Limitation of value due to those choices. In other words... It would be difficult to go from a humble job to be the CEO of some big corporation. It could also be difficult to go from having meaningless dates and short flings to being taken seriously as a love interest by a more spiritually advanced partner. It would be great if the past didn't pose a problem for the future, but it could be so. I have mixed feelings that are conflicting with each other. On the one hand I have always been romantic and vowed to do things my way and find true love and all that.

On the other hand, that approach made me miss on teenage dates, a high school sweetheart, etc. so when the years advance: 16, 17, 18, 19, 20, 21... and you see no progress following your romantic plan of absolute results you think: "Hey... I have waited quite a while and nothing seems to happen... Perhaps it's time to live a little?" And you do. And you find some happiness with your first girlfriend, and you realize that perhaps this was the right way all along... taking the little happiness that you can in a life that doesn't seem to grant absolute goals too often. Part of you keeps thinking that perhaps you are betraying the future love of your life that you still haven't met, but this is where my age and life experience play a big role: In my 37 years of life in this planet, I think I can safely say that I have never met my soulmate. So I could have been waiting and withering for something that would never come, wasting my life while doing so, or I could have enjoyed a bit and then apologize and atone for my promiscuous life at a later time if need be. Unfortunately this is one of those things that might vary from person to person, from culture to culture, and perhaps even from men to women. There is this deeply-rooted belief that women have it very easy to find sexual partners, and men need to prove themselves and be chosen, and all that, so a key that can open many locks is valuable and a lock that gets opened by any key is worthless. It is beyond my ability to tell you if such approach is correct, or if we can just dismiss it from the collective human culture with a few cynical words going against it, but the fact is that in my personal case I have had more luck being forgiven for my past partners by presenting the new ones with the things and skills that I learned along the way:

Her: "So you lived with three of your exes? And now you live with me? I am number four... How does this make me special? You are the first man I have ever lived with and...
Me: Aha, aha... Look what I learned to do with the second one, and look what the third one taught me...
Her: *a few orgasms later* "Ok, ok... I... I am gonna let this slide this time but... I want to find some place you never visited with them and make it ours".

I guess in a perfect world we would find the right partner and have no need nor interest in wasting time with lesser ones, but we live in an imperfect world and it's good that after we become physical with other human beings we can have some knowledge and skills to show for it. Experience at a physical, emotional, and sentimental levels can be the only thing that makes our promiscuity or baggage of past lovers seem like it will bring something positive to our current relationship. But yet again, this is just an opinion... When I am sure about something I tend to be adamant about it. In the topic of love and relationships I guess we are all more or less lost and making it as we go along through life. It's good to be humble about the things I don't know much about, and this is one of them.

On the topic of friendship I am quite specific. I recognize the inherent value of cohesion in society, and being nice to each other with the general objective of making life a bit easier and more agreeable. It's more efficient to be surrounded by prospective friends and having positive interactions than just a neutral or negative setting to develop as humans. It might seem like nice empty talk, but this approach has been proven to work in practical spheres like business, marketing, branding, etc. A well-regarded company is more likely to retain its customers and gain new ones. Positive interactions make us willing to repeat a purchase or service at a restaurant than neutral or negative ones. The same elementary results can be applied to life, with a few caveats that we could also find in businesses or services. Yes, being nice to customers tends to be the right way to go from a business point of view, unless they start ordering things that are not on the menu, complaining about everything, requesting change after change in their orders, breaking plates, bothering the other customers there, etc. then we would ask them to leave the restaurant as customers, or to leave our lives as friends.

Being friendly as a general concept is good if the environment is functional or even neutral. I have my doubts and reservations about being friendly in environments where that trait could be perceived as a weakness or as an invitation to relax the discipline. The best balance of those points that I have found was in martial arts. You can be joking like an idiot with a training friend, then totally focused on winning a combat against him without harming him or yourself, and then again jokingly messing around. In the Air Force I also saw a bit of that stuff. You could be playing basketball with your commanding officer at the gym, joking around, and looking straight ahead in perfect discipline the next morning. Perhaps the same concept could be applied to having a friendly demeanor as a default behavior, altering that to answer situations of danger or aggression, and coming back to the friendly mood right after that.

Friendship as a deeper concept of "people we bring into our inner circle" could be a bit more problematic. Depending on our own cultural baggage the difference between acquaintances and friends could be bigger or smaller. In some areas of the world it seems easier to make friends when you are traveling there, but I have always been a bit suspicious of that setting. I have the feeling that most people want to give a good impression of themselves, their social group, or their geographical area to visitors, so it's hard to know how much of that is genuine and how much is caused by your halo effect as a foreigner, or as an outsider. For a segment of the population it's cool to have certain foreign friends in specific circumstances because it increases their own social value in their group: "cool by association". This effect can be clearly appreciated in Japan, where most foreigners agree that they get approached by locals that treat them as exotic novelties, or collector items... but that doesn't translate into real deeper human connections. The same is true the other way around. When you are training karate, jujutsu, judo, or any other Japanese martial art, it may be nice if a local trainer compliments your technique, but if a Japanese one does the same you will be talking about it forever and ever, as if being born in the same country that created something gave a person more value and a real connection over it. "But Matt..." I hear you say "Doesn't it make sense that being in a country where something was invented, this person has had more contact with that activity and more knowledge about it as a direct result of that contact?" And yes, you would be right to think so, but if we remove that supposed close contact due to national connections, the reaction is the same. Any random inexperienced Japanese person could enter a Jujutsu class and say: "Hey kid, you are good!" and we would value that opinion more than if it were coming from a local trainer with years of experience.

A good way to try to determine how much of a friendship is genuine, and how much is due to circumstances external to that human connection is to analyze the rest of behaviors of a person. Especially if you are a girl, and even more so if you are mildly attractive. The idea that you can't keep female friends but male friends seem to be drawn to you because of your amazing personality is a lie that girls tell themselves all the time. If you can separate humans into two groups based on their genitals, and half of them don't get along with you but the other half follow you like puppies, it would be clear that the reason has to do with those genitals. As they grow up, girls are able to perform more tests on potential "friends"... Something like telling guys that they are married and have a son would make most super friendly friends be less interested in a friendship with you, unless you are incredibly hot and the effect of "cool by association" is at play even with a husband and a son: "The other female workers will see me joking and laughing with the hottest girl in the office and it will make me more desirable to them... even if the girl is married".

I am focusing on this from the point of view of being "the cool foreigner" or "the hot girl", but actually there are many circumstances where people tend to look for your friendship, approval, or just to be in your good graces for things other than how you are as a person. As soon as you have a bit of power in any social structure you can see this effect happening. In a game, moderating a forum, teaching a class, or wearing a military uniform around. People will react to you differently than when you are the same person in a different position. So I guess it would be fair to say that for genuine friendships we need to either eliminate those interferences from the equation (money, power, ulterior motives for approaching you, etc.) or we need to balance them with our own external interests and ulterior motives. So a hypothetical situation where we are appreciated as high value targets for friendship because we are cool exotic foreigners could balance out with our need for knowing locals to enjoy the country more. That could even be the base for a deeper human connection later on, but not for attractive girls... You still have to be on your guard for all those guys who use friendship as a way to get close enough to you to try enjoying the pleasures of your beauty. If you want to experience the real deal you can always go online to games, webs, and groups with a nick like: "Rupert_46" or "Fat_Mike_58". You will see that the interactions are more direct, nobody cares about your problems anymore, and the niceness goes down a few levels. I remember playing games where they would be berating me for playing like crap, I would say that I am a girl from Sweden or Norway, and everyone would apologize for being too harsh, offer ammunition or items, and become super nice and friendly all of a sudden... Why though? I was still the same person playing like crap? Then after the match you would get private messages asking how I am and invitations for future games... why though? Who would want such an awful player in their team? Well... call me mistrustful but I think it had a lot to do with projecting an idea of beautiful girl from a Scandinavian country playing so awfully probably from being too tired after modelling so much lingerie.

Another important point to consider is the presence of balancing external factors that could be mistaken by genuine friendship when actually they are just a version of the ulterior motives, but a less common one. You see, rich people, famous people, hot crazy people, etc. might need a calm environment in their lives, or being in contact with "real people", or roleplay for a while in a life that is not their own... This reference might be too obscure, or even irrelevant if you are reading this book in another century, but in this movie of Roberto Benigni, "Life is Beautiful" there is a good example of a famous important doctor before WW2 that likes to talk about riddles with the main character. During the war the main character is taken to a concentration camp and the doctor approaches him all worried. Instead of helping him with the imprisonment thing he wants to talk about a silly riddle, making the protagonist realize that this was the only interest of the doctor, even in the face of certain death for his "friend". And yeah, they were more like acquaintances in that movie but the point still stands... Some rich people just want "regular kids" to play with their own but you start noticing they don't really want them to get closer. At the end of the day you are providing a free service of "connection with the real life of the working class" that benefits them, but there are non-spoken limitations to such a friendship.

So as a general rule we can say that it is better to have allies than enemies, so it make sense to not be perceived as a danger to others, or as a possible source of conflict. The next step after being in this state of neutrality towards others can only be to evolve from neutral towards the positive side. Being careful to select the qualities and activities that will form the base for a friendship that will vary in intensity and attributions depending on the context, personalities, and needs of both friends. I mentioned qualities and activities because even if a person has qualities we find positive for us, if that person insists on meditating in silence and solitude in a temple in the mountains for most of the day during the next 12 years, it's going to be impossible to develop the friendship, engage in activities together, etc. It's an extreme example, I know, but it illustrates how time availability, need for common activities, and personal contexts can boost or soften the intensity of a friendship. We have all experienced situations in which good friends dropped a few levels in the friendship scale after moving to another city, changing schools, quitting gyms, or by any other circumstance that affected the general dynamic of the friendship: "We are still good friends, but I am moving to work in a North Pole Station for the next three years". Yes, the qualities are still there, it is still better to have an ally than to be neutral to that person, but the intensity would inevitably drop in terms of availability, common actions, help provided, etc. You can still communicate and enjoy having that person in your life, but it would come as no surprise to any of us that having a friend nearby is better than having him/her in the North Pole busy most of the time with experiments at what not. So for the people dealing in absolutes or maximalist approaches in life: Can we have/keep friends or relationships with people who don't live near us? Yes, we absolutely can, and we do all the time... Otherwise we would be constricting our ability to make friends or find other people attractive to our geographical location. In my case, you could already see that this didn't work for me for relationships. It wasn't until I started expanding my horizons that I had my first serious relationship, my first love stories, etc. The same can be true for friends and allies, but I guess we would all prefer to have our friends or love interests next to us and not in the North Pole.

So that's what I work with regarding friendship and intensity levels. If a friendship or a relationship is very strong, even decreasing the intensity level due to distance, for example, would still place it on top of anything else we could find limiting ourselves to our geographical location.

As a conclusion regarding the topic of friendship, we could say that as a general rule, establishing POSITIVE human connections is good for us. At the same time, "he who has a faithful friend holds a treasure" as the saying goes, and statistically speaking we don't find a ton of those treasures every week. The Romans used to say "don't let the friend of everybody become your friend", so those two points need to be carefully calibrated. Therefore it would stand to reason to conclude that it's not an easy task to find the right qualities, the right circumstances, and the right intensity to reach the highest levels of friendship. On top of that, maintaining too many intense friendship could deplete our personal time, our energy, or even conflict with other existing friendships. When we are young we have more friends than when we are older (the usual number is rarely above five friends for adults, and not many people would say they are happy about the intensity of the friendships in their lives). We could pay attention to other periods in human history where people lived with more social cohesion. We could also pay attention to other cultural settings to analyze the differences. If you fainted on the street, in some places they would leave you laying there, while in others a group of people would approach you to make sure you are alright. I believe the second place is a better environment to make deep human connections than the first one. I wouldn't like to have a friend in my life who said: "Today I saw someone fainting on the street and I went on my merry way because I didn't really care".

In my personal case, I was always amazed and impressed by the friendships and acquaintances my dad and his generation used to have. I remember walking around and everyone would nod, shake hands, shout from across the street, etc. Feeling part of a community and being recognized by others seemed like a double-edged sword when I was little and walking around with him. On the one hand this feeling that everyone felt better from being acquaintances that greet each other and exchange pleasantries seemed nice for the functioning of society, but it also seemed like a character weakness in a way. Like an inability to be happy without that acceptance and recognition from others around. In that spectrum we would have total individualism on one extreme, and social dependence in the other. Being a social junkie with a desperate need for friendship or social validation seems as dangerous as being a lonesome individualist unable to find anything positive or valuable in any other human being on the planet. Managing those two extremes and getting away from them seems like the right way to go unless you can fully function by needing people all the time, or by not needing them at all now or in the future.

CHAPTER FIVE: Things I learned in my trips

A few of them I have already mentioned... I try to travel with the mentality that things will go wrong to try and anticipate any possible setbacks. I carry my plane and train tickets in the phone and tablet as images and as PDF documents. I also print them if it's about flights. I have already tested this habit a few times: The screen of your phone breaks during your trip (including the protective cover) and the reader can't catch the code on your phone. You could pay an extra fee for printing the ticket or... exactly: the tablet.

I carry the phone numbers of some friends and relatives written in paper inside my wallet in case I lose the phone or it breaks down. I also carry the phone numbers I would have to call to cancel my credit cards, as well as a couple of addresses, my sizes for clothes written on a paper, and a few other items that have proven handy but it would make you think I am crazy.

First of all my keyring is a USB lantern. It's always useful to have your own source of light in any situation, especially with those toilets where the lights are automatic, or entering buildings where the entrance lights are off or so... Yes, I am aware that mobile phones have lantern functions and I use them too. This type of keyring is more for cases like when I was living in Ireland and the lights went out for hours in my neighborhood due to some storm. I connected the keyring to an external battery for phones and tablets and I could function normally around the house. I guess I could have lasted for several days considering the amount of electricity I was using. At some point I had a shower, hanging the contraption from the real lamp of the bathroom. Which takes me to my next item in my wallet: Dental floss. I carry around 2 meters of it (7 feet? 12 knees? 19 elbows? I dunno... really... go metric please... this is insane) and it has many uses. In a rented apartment where there was no space to dry my clothes, I tied it between 2 points and I could hang my trousers, sweater, t-shirt, underwear, and socks). Dental floss is sturdier than it looks and it has also helped me once when I needed to pass something to a colleague one floor below. Instead of spending time going to her, wait for the elevator, or walk up and down the stairs, I asked her to go to the window on the right side of her classroom, I put the item in a plastic bag, and I lowered it with the dental floss. The last time I used it, it was to tie an item a bit better to a trolley that I use sometimes to go shopping like an old lady. The weirdest thing I have done with it is to use it as an improvised net to play some sort of volleyball-tennis mixture with a ball of rolled-up socks.

I also carry plasters in my wallet (4 of them) that I can use to stick things together (a note for example, it wouldn't be the first time), and in my keyring there is also a big metal clip: one of those hardened ones that don't bend easily. To be honest I have only used it as a hook to pick some keys that fell down a rain hole, and as a support point to tie the dental floss to, but I guess I could also pick something easy like a file cabinet or a mailbox with it.

When I travel I take all sorts of movies, shows, pdf magazines, downloaded documentaries, ebooks, radio programs as audio files, offline games, emulators, etc. I always plan my trips for hours and hours of boredom, so wherever I am I can switch from one activity to the next alternating between the tablet and the phone. It's better to have more than you need, than to run out of entertainment waiting for a plane that will be ready in 4 hours. And why so many formats? Well, I have noticed that my eyes get tired after a few hours, so the music, the audiobooks, and the audio programs allow me to have my eyes closed so they can rest. I use every opportunity to charge my phone. When I say every opportunity I mean looking for a USB plug when the battery is at 94%. That extra 6% can mean one extra hour of audio or more. I go around the airports or waiting areas of bus/train stations crouching, looking under the seats, and all that stuff, trying to locate hidden sockets of those that are covered by a lid the same color as the floor... oh... they won't fool me with one of those!

I acquire my water bottles after passing the security control. I calculate for 50% more water than I would usually need so that if I need to be in a hurry when I arrive to my transit or destination, I can run around without worrying about being thirsty later. I resist the urge to get rid of an empty bottle if I haven't acquired a new bottle or two depending on the length of my trip. Water helps us against fatigue, and it can mean the difference between a pleasant trip and a horrible one.

If I have to sleep at an airport, or I see the risk of falling asleep I always use two alarms and with plenty of time before my flight. I select vibration, lights, loud volume... I have several tricks to make my sleep more comfortable. We all have to trade our dignity for a comfortable rest at some point of our traveling adventures. The first trick is to acquire a newspaper since that type of material insulates quite well from the cold floor and will be cleaner than coming directly into contact with it. I may also use one of those big plastic bags for garbage cans that they carry in the cleaning trolleys; yes, I steal those if I have the chance. The only item I might consider stealing, I think. I will take out a few clothing items to use as pillow and extra warmth together with my coat or jacket, and after that I will look for a desolate place without people passing by. An area under construction where I don't see any movement, a bunch of piled-up trolleys, or if I am feeling bold enough I will go around then non-common areas holding a paper and if someone stares at me for too long I will approach them with a dumb smile on my face and ask about the VIP lounge. If I can't find one of these places I will create an exclusion area with a suitcase trolley and another one to occupy space or avoid direct access to me. Among the coolest things I ever managed to do, but just once due to pure luck of matching designs, was the time I put my suitcase in a horizontal position on the trolley, one coat on top of it to soften the weight for laying on it, and then strapped two belts joining a chair and the trolley, giving me enough surface with the seat and the trolley to have the closest thing to a bed one can make at an airport. I know there are people who carry sleeping mats and inflatable pillows, but I guess the space the mat would take is too much for my philosophy of traveling with as little baggage as possible to move around easily. If I ever had a trip of several transits with a few days at the airports of different countries I would probably prepare better and include a mat as well, but as pillow I prefer to put clothes inside a bag and then put a t-shirt on top, or something like that.

The locks for my bags and suitcases always have numbers. I am a lock-picking enthusiast myself, and it takes me much more time to guess a 4-digit combination than to pick the weakest locks in existence. The cons have to do with airport security usually breaking the combination locks if they are in a hurry and they can't open them through pressure applied on the sides or sliding a metal layer inside the holes. In other words... if your combination lock is too good and you packed cables in your suitcase, it might not be there when you land.
A pair of earplugs can be a gift from heaven if you are on a flight with a crying baby or if you want to sleep at a busy airport. That's when the alarms with vibration play a role. Putting the phone inside your hood, secured with a thread or the dental floss tied to the cover if you must. If you don't want to travel with expensive earphones but you like the concept of noise reduction, remember you can get a pair of ear protectors like the ones they

use for shooting. The cheaper versions are just a few coins and they can be tossed away without feeling you have lost too much.

Another item people usually forget, besides the secondary pair of cable headphones, is the double jack in case someone on the flight wants to share your movie, video, music, etc. But it will also give you an extra life when the left headphone stops working, and the left headphone on the secondary pair also stops working... It will allow you to combine them both inserting them in both jacks to get a functioning pair of headphones again. If you ever get locked inside a door, remember you can try to move the metal bolt back with two credit cards. One moves it to the right, the other one holds it in place once the movement is completed, before the first card tries to move it a bit more. It can also slide the mechanism inside if you are in the room, but it rarely works if you are outside so that's how I know this advice might take you out of some troubles but it will not turn you into a burglar. It only works inside rooms with crappy doors, not in buildings or houses from the outside.

Keep in mind the items and services an airport can provide for you. Besides charging all your electronics, you can dry something quickly in the machine inside the bathrooms, toilet paper and paper towels can come in handy for cleaning the area where you will sleep or sit, and the hand soap can also be collected in a travel bottle for future uses. I know these are extreme scenarios, but being prepared never hurt anyone. About which electronics to charge, remember the power bank should go next after your phone, and yes, before I called power banks "external batteries" but the term didn't catch on, so I come back to the fold. Another thing related to the services of an airport and what they can provide for you: keep in mind that some of them will have this office where they give you back the VAT of your shopping receipts inside a country if you are not a resident of that country, so it can be a way to get some of your money back if you are lucky with the requirements.

And about the things that can happen inside an airport, I have the habit of never making any jokes near airport workers, especially security staff. It must be tiresome having to frisk someone and getting lines like: "I hope my girl doesn't get too jealous mweh, heh, heh, heh". I usually act like a robot in those situations. I provide informative short answers, polite smiles, and I open my suitcase without hesitation as soon as they request it. I go to the desks and security checks as soon as I am allowed to do so. I prefer waiting inside the boarding area or the gates rather than outside. Even with these sensible habits I found myself short on time in two different airports... imagine how long the lines for the security checks were.

I never buy anything inside a plane (even inside an airport if I can avoid it). It's true that my longest flight has only been 5 hours, but I prefer carrying my own food from some local supermarket. I don't mind spending the same amount of money or more, but getting my money's worth of food and sweets. Unless money is not an issue for you whatsoever, every little thing you do to stretch your budget will allow you more pocket money when you land, or extra funds for your next trip. This type of mentality goes in a neat pack together with any other financial strategy that helps me do more with the same funds. I avoid lavish expenses if they don't carry extra value that is closely related to their price. In other words, I might end up spending the same or even more than another person but in a combination of two trips instead of one.

So now for some things I learned living in different countries. In London I learned or refreshed the lesson that money is important. If instead of saving for three months I had saved for longer and had sold a few items to get even more funds, I would have been able to open my own bank account there instead of depending on other people. Studying the bus and metro lines before using them was a good way to not look like a lost ducky in a new city. Carrying passport photos is always a good idea for documents and interviews. This was the first time I realized that it's good to have all the possible documents you might need to get something you want, which also includes any card or membership that can provide me with some benefit. The

International Students Identity Card, travel insurance policies provided by my credit card company, discount stuff for fast food restaurants, etc. navigating through a new big city with some extra cards to play can boost your confidence and feel that you have a firm grasp on the system. In my jobs I tried to be efficient, not give many troubles, and act professional and in a hurry when the bosses were looking, but waste time whenever I could. If a company pays well I give a good performance. If a company pays minimum wage and I see colleagues getting fired left and right as soon as the workload decreases, I assume regardless of how well I work I will suffer the same fate. That type of job wasn't a context in which some guy was going around with a notebook writing down who was professional and who wasn't. They needed 20 people for a temp job, the job was over and goodbye. They never called any of my colleagues again and I never saw anyone being offered a permanent contract. We had exceptional workers and people who had been raised with the idea that working hard and showing what you are worth will make your bosses notice you, etc. It didn't happen. In fact some of the best workers left with some of the worst and some of the average ones as soon as the workflow decreased in those companies... It was completely arbitrary, so giving your best and putting 110% effort, and all that nonsense would have only burnt me out and drained my energy. Extra pay, extra effort. Minimum wage, minimum effort.

London taught me that you can build a cool city, or a cool country that can change in a matter of a few decades. In the span of a human lifetime you can see everything you knew and admitted as eternal changing drastically to a point where the original idea can't be easily recognized anymore. Every single old person with whom I spoke about London, their lives, or their memories kept confirming the idea that things were evolving for the worst. This may, of course, be a bias where their years of youth and their childhoods are idealized and all that, but sometimes the memories were as fresh as 12 years ago. I had the feeling that these traditional British people were like a bucket of yellow paint, and immigrants like myself were blue paint. By our attitudes, cultures, and behaviors, drop after drop of blue paint managed to turn the yellow bucket into a green one. I guess it was good and cosmopolitan for some things, but it also left me wondering if by being part of something you can change it so fundamentally that you destroy it by the sheer logic of numbers. Don't get me wrong, I wasn't going around London whipping and punishing myself for polluting the place with my foreign habits, but to put it into perspective, I felt as if someone had found a quiet garden by the river where you could hear birds singing and the relaxing flow of water, and then they had invited there all their friends, relatives, and acquaintances to the point where you could no longer hear any birds, nor relax, and the plastics and packages of half-eaten food were now covering the beautiful grass. Once again, I don't consider myself a self-hating traveler or anything like that but London was like a festival of classical music where one of the groups insisted on playing heavy metal, while another group was obsessed with jazz, and another group went around saying they hated music and festivals and they wish the place became a copy of their place of origin.

I was the strange kid who went to public parks to practice martial arts and exercises with wooden sticks, receiving a nod of approval by a Caribbean guy with loud music, and the horrifying looks of an old British lady walking around with her grandchildren. I have no idea how much I should have changed and adapted to fit in with the environment, but I can honestly tell you that I wasn't one of the worst cases of foreign influence in that land.

In the Baltics I learned a new set of habits and behaviors. At a deeper level than before I mean. Everything was different in a familiar way. There were supermarkets but the products were totally different. Although it would have been possible to go the extra mile and pretend that you were still back in your country, eating the same food and all that, the more I tried the more things I found appealing, so I ended up using different clothes, becoming used to different products, having different habits at the beach, in my work, for having fun... There I changed so many parts of my life that I really felt like roleplaying the life of another person: "Uh! Look at me! I am going to take this cheese cream with pieces of shrimps, put it over this bread I have never seen, add some meat I had never eaten, and drink kefir near the frozen lake where I made a hole on the ice for fishing!" The whole scenario was bizarre compared to what my life had been up until that point. I saw winters where people died of hypothermia if they drank too much and fell asleep after a night out... It was something really unusual for me. The social interactions, the foreign speech everywhere, the different habits... it all made me understand the limitations that our social environment puts on us. From being politely encouraged to improve my English a few years before, to being proclaimed as the best speaker anyone had ever met up until that point. From being ignored in my country, to being complimented on a regular basis being the exact same person. It was shockingly different.

In the Baltics I had to deal with a constant personal complex. The idea that I was not as successful as other people even after having gone so fast from private tutor to university teacher. I kept seeing the prices at the expensive shops, people entering there in large groups, and the overall consumption habits everyone seemed to have, and I started feeling perhaps I was being cheated. Perhaps their salaries were higher and I needed to find a better job, with a higher income, and all that. I would learn the reality a bit later: While I was saving 40-50% of my salary and money from private classes, more than 63% of the population in that small Baltic country were addicted to consumer credits. Their bank accounts were bare and empty, and not only that, they were fueling their consumption desires with loans, personal credits, and installments that had a high interest rate. The country would be one of the worst performers during the crisis that would occur 2 years later. In retrospective you feel that everything makes sense, but there were weekends I was going around thinking: "Wow... that guy works with me and he just left that expensive shop with two bags full of clothes... How does he do it? Are my bosses cheating me?" And the simple answer was that we were earning the same, or perhaps I was earning a bit more if we add the private lessons, but they were pretending to be rich with money that wasn't theirs.

I guess my attitude towards savings, financial stability, and all that was already there since I was a child. They explain you that the banks give you money if you already have money with them and you think it's too good to be true. They explain you that you can buy small portions of successful companies and then sell them to make a profit and you think: "It can't be this easy... otherwise everyone would be getting some extra cash putting their money on companies that keep growing and growing... There must be some fine print they are not telling us". And yes, the fine print is that even the biggest safest companies could collapse after a century of history if you are not paying attention to social changes, consumer habits, new laws, and all that stuff. Nevertheless, going from a comfortable position with two small businesses when I was little, to a situation where it was difficult to make ends meet just 15 years later probably sharpened my idea that the world was out to get me and that you can be on top one moment, and declining a bit later heading towards a hard financial situation.

There is another powerful reason to have savings and to be able to produce extra income, even if it's little. I can only feel truly free when I can quit a job if they ask me to break some ethical red line of mine, or if the job is making me miserable or something like this. It's hard for everyone that doesn't have some security and reserves to draw from, and it was hard for me too when I started working, saving, and all that. I can't say that I am totally safe right now, because for example, I have savings equal to 35 minimum monthly salaries in my country. I still consider myself poor because if something happened to my house, or I wanted to leave it for some reason, I could only afford three or four years of humble rent, basic food and expenses without getting another source of income. In past times it may have been enough, but nowadays being three years away from homelessness doesn't really sound like staring at the horizon from a high ivory tower of financial safety... It feels more like a countdown of 36 months before bankruptcy. And yes, you may think I am being too dramatic because that capital could be producing some benefits since it doesn't need to be spent all at once, and you would be right but: Can those benefits pay the rent, food, and basic expenses of a person? The answer is no, so even in the best-case scenario I would just be giving myself an extra year while having to reconstruct my savings salary after salary in the event of finding a stable job later on.

There would be more radical alternatives like changing my place of residence to a country where the money I have, and the small profits it would produce can last me for a longer time, or maybe even sustaining myself, but it would be one of those final nails in the coffin of my sanity probably: "Hi friends! I have moved to Cambodia to avoid homelessness, I don't know how my life went so wrong, but the weather is nice and they say there hasn't been a military coup since 1997! Fingers crossed!" So from all aspects and points of view it seems of capital importance to reach as much financial security as possible to be able to resist hard times, unexpected expenses, unemployment, etc. What's the right amount? I have no idea about the circumstances of other people. Sometimes I have the feeling that everyone is inheriting properties from some distant relative, or being able to ask for a huge amount of money from their parents to try different business ventures or stuff like that. I guess when we don't have anyone to ask for help, the right amount of savings should be higher and only be relaxed as we cover enough prospective risks and problems.

As a general rule I would say that you should calculate the number of years you are supposed to live if you reach the average life expectancy in the area of the world where you plan to reside. So in my case, I am 37 now, let's say I have to live 50 more years. My first absolute goal would be to cover all the normal expenses for those 50 years living a middle-class life. Your goals will depend on your habits, if you drive a car, hobbies, etc. but having the bare minimum expenses covered for the rest of your life seems like a very reasonable goal to work with. If with the money you already have you are able to produce enough money to cover this year's expenses and save a bit, that would be a balance point where one could relax a bit. It would be mentally and spiritually exhausting to go through life thinking your doom might come soon when you have acquired the equivalent of 10 years' worth of regular expenses. You will only need one year of expenses to work with and the other 9 can keep producing more cash, so relaxing gradually seems healthy.

Why do I consider this number so important whether you reach it or not? Because if you make your calculations, add a bit more for extra circumstances, travels, or improving your quality of life in the long run, you will see that most people are greedy without a reason. Once they have surpassed well beyond their optimal amount of savings, they keep obsessing about the subject as if they had started saving just last week. The existence of billionaires or even multimillionaires is also a bit puzzling from a practical point of view. How many years do they expect to live? How much money does a human being require to keep him/her happy with his living standards? I am not involved in an exercise of proletarian demagogy to point at the richest among us with inquisitorial intent. I am honestly wondering if some of these people have ever realized that we work mostly to earn the means of our survival and wellbeing. Once those two things are assured for us and for our close circle, isn't it redundant to keep burning time and energy working instead of pursuing different activities and accumulating pleasant life experiences? And yes, I fully understand that for some people their jobs are a source of pleasure, status, validation, etc. but isn't a job a collection of activities that could be performed under more fulfilling circumstances and with deeper goals than the accumulation of wealth? Again, from a position of pure rational balance: If I had the next 50 years of my life paid for, and then you doubled that amount, or tripled it in case I want to live spending much more... after which point could we say that I was being illogical for insisting on working more and more hours once I can clearly sustain myself with the wealth I have already accumulated? 3% of 2 million dollars gives you 60,000 dollars per year plus the initial amount. Take into account the point in time in which I am writing this, adjust for inflation, etc. and think why if 2 million dollars seem to be enough to live a comfortable life, there are people obsessed with acquiring more and more past that point. Fine, maybe they like the finer things in life, let's double it or triple it: Why don't they stop working and stressing after reaching 4 or 6 million dollars?

I have always thought that greed without points of reference is one of the reasons why some things don't work as well as they should with individuals and societies. Greed might be embraced to fulfill certain financial objectives regarding not being homeless, traveling a few times per year, or acquiring a comfortable home, or two, or three. However past that point greed becomes useless and detrimental for the individuals that don't enjoy the benefits of their wealth, and for societies that see the same people occupying the same positions longer than they should have.

These and some other things I learned in the Baltics, so when the financial crisis of 2009 struck them, debts swallowed a lot of companies, families, and individuals. I have always seen debt as the downfall of many national and personal economies, and accumulated wealth as a safety net for the uncertain future, and I am a single guy without children so imagine the extent of my surprise when I saw older colleagues with children and responsibilities drowning in personal loans and consumerism. It was beyond my comprehension to see them place short-term satisfaction derived from the acquisition of products in front of the minimum standards of financial stability for themselves and their loved ones. If I ever get global dictatorial powers expect a lot of courses and seminars for the population about the importance of savings.

Going now to the things I learned in Denmark. I saw the difference between that country and Sweden. I have applied to endless Swedish universities and got rejected mostly for not knowing Swedish. Keep in mind that I am a linguist and I would be teaching my native language there just like I did in the other countries. The Swedish requirements were insanely difficult to meet, and their bureaucracy is specific to that particular country. I would often wonder why Danish universities scored so well in international rankings while Swedish ones were so far away especially in parameters like internationalization. In Denmark I had my answer. Being hired by the University of Copenhagen was one of the most pleasant professional experiences I have ever had. Everything was clear, direct, efficient, and at the end of my contract the reviews for my work there had been fantastic. You could see there was a specific attention to achieve the best results. Sweden was the exact opposite... You would send an email and the answer would come in Swedish. You would apply to some place and they would ask you about some paper or local certificate you could only get by living there. It was a bureaucratic nightmare that added to the other bureaucratic nightmares the country has to offer on its own: "Oh! Nice house near the coast, I would like to buy it... Wait, what do you mean I already have to be living in the municipality to buy a weekend house there? Why would I want to buy a house at a place where I already live? Who made it legal to discriminate buyers based on their place of residence? Oh... ok, I will rent some apartment then... I really want to spend a few months enjoying the country... Wait, what do you mean I have to sign up on a list? I have money to rent an apartment and I would like an apartment from... you know... the free market... I come loaded from Denmark... Take my money!" All those bureaucratic hurdles from Sweden contrasted sharply with the pleasant system the Danish have created, so one couldn't help but understanding why one country is growing so fast while the other one is losing ground in comparison to its neighbors and to its glorious past.

In the Balkans I had a great time despite feeling like a hero of epic proportions for giving back the money from wrong change at a shop or a bus. I was basically just having fun with the girl, playing video games, and training in their beautiful parks. The prices were affordable (at least back then), and I had to write my doctoral thesis, so the experience was necessary and welcome. The environment would have been normal if not for a few things that reminded you that a few years ago, many of those people you encountered on the street would have been shooting at other people. It dawned on me when I paid attention to my butcher's tattoos. The guy used to try his English skills with me and we would have conversations about video games, board games, movies, and stuff like that. He wasn't in any particular hurry to give me my sausages, pljeskavica (a very tasty meat for burgers), or my chicken... so we would talk about this and that. One day I asked about his tattoos and they turned out to be from a group called the Arkan's Tigers. After researching a bit and watching the videos I understood that even the nicest person you could meet in the part of the world at that time might have been killing other people or doing horrible things just a few years earlier (by horrible things I mean war crimes of any kind, not just participating in a military conflict). It might sound hypocritical considering I also volunteered to join the military in my country, and it probably is... but one couldn't help wondering who was the real person behind any middle-aged guy you met in an area that had lived a civil war not long ago. Was this a good person forced to live exceptional circumstances, or was this a bad person trying to make his way through life in peace times?

As a general note, if you want to dig a bit deeper in that conflict, but not too much because it's boring and all that... I recommend you to check the articles about the main figures of that war. One doesn't know if to laugh or cry, but it's all quite unusual and a bit pathetic. One of the main generals became a builder who would often get told how much he resembled that guy from the TV news from years ago. Another one, president of the country I think, grew a beard and opened a clinic specialized in natural remedies. I don't want to spoil you the rest of the surprises, but it would have been funny to hear the guy fixing your walls murmuring: "Oh... He doesn't like this tone of yellow for the bedroom... Meh! I used to order artillery strikes. I once captured a NATO company and held them hostages... I don't need to take this crap!"

I visited countries like The Netherlands, Germany, Czech Republic, Poland a few times, and what not... but I didn't really live in those countries so I didn't acquire any knowledge that could be passed onto you. Perhaps just the general feeling that we could establish anywhere in the world if we manage to have the basic services covered, the basic problems solved, and all that. You may think that the language barrier is an obstacle, and you may be right... but even carrying a list of words, or learning a few of them to communicate basic concepts could be enough to function at a very basic level. Between those small efforts, the translation apps for text, and all the other stuff, it's easier and easier to move around, especially with some money. I would also recommend you to keep in mind the services other people can provide for you. In countries where the exchange rates are in your favor you could benefit from contacting some Philology student in a forum and saying: "Hey, I will pay you this amount for coming with me to check apartments for rent in the next couple of days". Boom. One less problem to worry about. In any place where the rule of law is respected (including property rights and all) we could probably create our own bubble to feel at home: movies, music, shows, sport, nature... It's easier and easier to make some place "your own" if the basic rules for a civilized society are respected. Investigating a bit about the news, laws, and personal stories of other people who moved to a certain place you are interested in could be the key to decide if you would be happy there or not. In any case, moving to another country doesn't have to be forever. You can move to the next, and the next, until you find your place; provided that you are not burning your savings while doing so.

Ireland taught me a few more things about bureaucracy. It's an amazing country with nice people. Remember when I told you before that it would be advisable to live in a place where if you fell on the street people would approach to help you? Ireland is probably one of those places, but it might suffer the same problem nowadays than London a couple of decades ago. Too many immigrants like me going there at the same time might affect the place and change it beyond repair *checks the criminality statistics of the last years* yep, maybe it would be good to have a public debate about this subject before it happens the same as in London. And if they decide it's better for people like me not to go there, well tough luck for me I guess, but at least we will still have Ireland unspoiled and beautiful as it always was.

One thing that shocked me is that whenever they look abroad for inspiration for some law, policy, or way of doing things, they end up looking at the UK rather than at the continent. It's probably due to historical reasons and the influence of the returning emigrants, so you find things that can only be found there... and in UK, which makes it weird in conversations where they complain about the historical relations between both countries: "Oh you should have seen what they did to us in the time of my great-grandparents... The humiliations that..." "Aha... have you thought about driving in the normal side of the road like the rest of the world instead of driving like the UK?" "Err... no... no... It's fine like this I guess". So the result is like a small version of the UK where the houses look really similar, the habits are really similar, the road system is also similar, etc. and it is surprising at many levels.

Ireland was a bit of a test for me because living there was difficult. I was in the north west of the country. Finding a house was difficult, opening a bank account was difficult, going for a walk was difficult... Let me explain this in detail. There is a shortage of houses for rent in certain areas. The Irish universities keep growing but without taking care of the housing needs of students or teachers, so a small town near a university can have everything occupied without too many difficulties for it. The prices are higher than in other countries but still affordable, but finding a house took me a few weeks and it was a bit of a hassle. Nothing compared to opening a bank account there, though. There are laws in place within the European Union for residents to open bank accounts in other countries as if they were in their own, however for reasons beyond my understanding all those nice ideas of a union of countries crash against the harsh realities of individual members of the union that insist on doing whatever they like as if they hadn't agreed to follow certain common protocols.

I had opened accounts in other countries before. Passport, signing a few documents, deposit some money and done. In Ireland they required to have a bill on your name, but it couldn't be a phone bill, or some delivery, no. It had to be some utility bill so I had to ask the landlord to put one of HIS bills on my name, which he politely declined because then changing it back would be a problem and blah, blah. I thought about getting some internet package for the house, but the prices were oddly high for what they were offering. I managed to open an account in the bank branch inside my university campus. It was easy and quite fast. This was the same bank where they had told me at another office that it was impossible without a utility bill. The same bank that was rescued during the 2009 crisis together with a few other banks I had visited. Rescued as in... they had required public money from Europe for not being able to sustain themselves and being profitable. One would imagine that in such circumstances they would be happy to welcome new clients to deposit their salaries month after month, but it was more or less the opposite: "ugh... a client... what a drag... do you have a gas bill on your name a week after arriving to the country? No? Awww... tough luck". After opening that first bank account I went to a second bank that had rejected me a month earlier, but now with another bank's balance statement I could open an account there without any trouble. Since then a few online banks had popped up in the market, but in any case it's sad when companies don't understand how to stay profitable and efficient. Customers = Good.

When I said before that having a walk was also difficult I kinda meant it. In some cities and towns I visited the sidewalks would suddenly stop without a reason, as the roads went on... So I thought I could go to the beach having a run and I found myself in the middle of a road without any place to go on running except by invading the space of the cars. I tried to go to a famous mountain and the same story. Even walking lanes outside public parks could suddenly finish without any reason for it. It was as if some urbanist had decided: "You know what? That's enough sidewalk for you pedestrians... buy a car if you want to move farther from this particular and random point!"

Although Irish people were nice and cool, I left the country with the feeling that perhaps it was harder to live there than I had imagined. Basic things like receiving medical attention had added extra steps and fees that made everything less inclusive. To visit a doctor you need to register at some place first and pay 50 euros, just for registering... with a doctor... I don't know if you are reading this in the 23rd century but as I write this, 50 euros was enough for the grocery shopping of 10 days more or less. That money just for putting your name inside some register. I left the place without registering myself, of course, partly because of principles and partly because I was healthy and stingy and I figured I wouldn't be needing medical services that much. After registering, each visit to the doctor had an extra fee, meaning that you had to pay again for the privilege of using public health services that you had already paid for with your taxes. It's becoming harder and harder to argue with private healthcare users when you compare costs and services.

It was at that point when I thought I was paying too many taxes for the things I was receiving, so I started looking for agreements, backdoors, and laws to recover most of my taxes based on the fact that I wasn't a resident because I didn't reside more than half a year in the country in a given year. How is that, you ask? An academic year starts in September, so that year you only live there 4 months. The next year you just have to leave the country before the 30th of June so that technically you haven't resided there for more than half a year, and you can claim refunds as a non-resident scholar. To be entirely honest with you, I wouldn't even have bothered to find such weird laws and regulations if I had felt that the country had my back and I was getting my money's worth of services and stuff. I don't ask much... streets to walk on, a few cops to keep the peace, and knowing that the country cares about my health and doesn't see it as an opportunity to charge me money. I know that if you are reading this from a country where the hospitals work in some other way you may be having troubles understanding what I mean. Think of it this way: when a house is on fire, someone calls the firefighters and they put out the fire. You don't need to hire firefighting services yourself, or worry if your type of fire will pick their interest, or ponder about the limits of your fire coverage. If there is a fire you expect the guys in red trucks to come and extinguish it. If there is a crime being committed you are not expected to have thought about it before and call your personal security company to see if they can help... you call the general cops that everyone uses and they do their job. So likewise if you collapse on the street you get taken to the city hospital and they should help you with whatever you need so that you don't feel that your life is worthless and your health is only a merchandise to extract money from you at your weakest moments.

"But Matt!" I hear you say, "Why should I pay for the unhealthy life habits of other citizens with my taxes?" Well, random hypothetical person, because the alternative is letting them die and that creates external problems and ramifications that are hard to see at a first glance. For starters, nobody uses this argument with the cops or the firefighters: "Why should I pay with my taxes the bad decision of that guy building his house out of wood instead of concrete?" "Why should I subsidize with my taxes your habit of going out to rough bars at night where the probability of getting in a fight or requiring assistance from the cops in any way is much higher? I don't even drink..." "Why should I subsidize the rescue services in mountainous terrain? So you like climbing high rocks, you get stranded up there in the snow and we all have to pay for it? So unfair!" "Why should I pay for hurricane relief funds in other areas or countries? I don't even live there!" I guess I made my point extensively clear. If someone is worried about the unhealthy habits of their fellow citizens it's time to think about parks, sports activities for the elderly, and subsidizing basic nutritional products like porridge, milk, eggs, chicken, apples, carrots, etc. And even if after taking every possible measure to make it easy for people to ride bicycles, eat well, walk around, etc. we still have a segment of the population that insists on spoiling their health, I suppose it would fall under the same category as people who have houses made with flammable materials, or people who climb high mountains, or people who need to be rescued by the police from their nocturnal habits. "But Matt!" I hear you say again, "The doctors and medical professionals deserve to be paid accordingly to their worth!" Well first of all, I didn't see doctors in Denmark, Ireland, Spain, or UK living in bad conditions. They are comfortable middle class and even upper-middle class. I want to think we all should be paid according to our value as professionals (the value we generate for the system as some say), but when those payments come from the health needs of other human beings, the whole argument becomes a bit shaky... I am sorry I can't afford this procedure with you doctor, you are an excellent professional that deserves a thousand praises for your acquired skills... Where should I go to die? Can I do it here or quietly at home so I don't bother with my health issues?" It is however an unnecessary argument when we consider that medicine is a vocation and if someone becomes a physician caring more about money than about saving lives, perhaps the profession can do without them.

Anyhow, having to pay for registering just in case I need to see a doctor in the future got me annoyed and made me reduce the taxes I had to pay. Everything exquisitely legal, but judging by my own example I am willing to bet there is a segment of the population who are constantly getting the message that without money nobody cares about them, or their health... so it's hard to drive those people away from greed and consumerism when they are living in a society that only provides them with goods and services if they have money to pay for them. It makes societies into a jungle where if someone has success they might have the temptation of caring about their own needs after years and years of receiving the message that nobody cares about them if they don't pay for it. I like that the firefighters come when there is a fire, or a kitty up on a tree without blaming pet owners or people who don't build with brick and mortar.

I don't think I can be considered a mentally-retarded idealist for believing that simple things like seeing fountains where you can drink for free, benches where you can sit to rest, or knowing if you have a serious problem you will get the helping hand of your fellow human beings dressed in different uniforms or without them, can make you look at society as a team effort where we are all living our individual stories and coping with our own struggles, but we are able to snap out of all that when a child gets lost, or an old lady faints on the street, or someone falls on hard times for reasons objectively beyond their own conscious efforts to fail on purpose. Societies work more efficiently when those acquired habits have been interiorized and accepted as positive for us and for everyone else. We would still have to face death, heartbreaks, evil, and hardships, but we would do so knowing there is an underlying unspoken agreement that we are all in this together, and we become better when we are a force for good when the exceptional circumstances require it.

CHAPTER SIX: About teaching

Teaching is a human function that we have made into a specific profession to maximize results and specialize our societies. It would be the same as taking care of someone recovering in a bed: as humans we have the ability of doing it ourselves, even if there are also professional nurses and medical assistants that can perform the required tasks at a specialized level.

A weird introduction for the topic, I know, but starting from this point it's easier to understand that anyone can be a teacher because we can all transmit knowledge to others. You can do it better or worse, improve your skills, and adapt your mentality to different environments and students but at the end of the day, teaching is something we can all do because we are part of the same nature where adult lions teach younger cubs to hunt, or where baby giraffes learn how to move or interact with other members of their species by following examples and copying them. Humans might have more advanced requirements for some subjects and activities, but the main mechanism is there. So if you ever wanted to become a teacher, or just due to the possibility that you may have to teach something to someone at some point in your life, here are some pointers from a guy that has been doing this for years, in different settings, different countries, and different subjects:

a) You are a source of knowledge, not a person anymore. This mindset has always helped me be a bit more successful than my colleagues. My mission is to transmit knowledge to others in an efficient and clear way. During the transmission of knowledge and information, anything that deviates from that mission is going to decrease the quality. Having said this, personal examples might still be valuable as part of the teaching process, as well as elements like brief jokes that should be aimed at empathizing with the students, making them relaxed, or reminding them that we are all on the same boat with a certain subject. So a quick joke related to the subject would be useful, a brief comment about how it took you a long time to understand a certain topic might be encouraging, but complaining for 10 minutes about how awful the weather is might be subtracting time and knowledge from the class and decreasing your performance. "But Matt, before you said something about minimum wage getting minimum effort and..." Yes, yes... I remember what I said. I am now explaining you what I learned for optimal performance. Do we need optimal performance in all settings and areas of life where we will be teaching something to someone? Clearly not... I fool around a lot when I am explaining something unimportant to a friend for example, and I am a precise machine of knowledge transmission when I am preparing students for some official examination. You are the one with the personal choice and responsibility to determine the degree of commitment and excellence you want to apply when you are teaching. However as a general rule it's good to be able to select different levels of performance and to switch off the "me, me, me, this is about me" mentality and switch on the "I am a knowledge machine calibrated for optimal results" one.

b) The student needs to be willing to learn. It seems like something obvious, but not even the best teacher could transmit knowledge efficiently to a student who covers his ears and sings: "la, la, la" while we explain stuff. This is an extreme example, of course, but it helps us see the importance of motivating the students, explaining why the subject is relevant, describing the things that can be done with that knowledge, etc. The motivation needs to be based on real facts and accurate descriptions because otherwise we risk alienating the students if they perceive dishonesty in our words. Passive knowledge can also be transmitted but as you can probably guess it has just a fraction of the efficiency. We could be forced to watch cricket matches (the "sport" not the animal) being totally uninterested by it, ignoring the events before us as much as we can, and yet after hours of doing so we would still be able to identify the sticks, the action, the gear worn by the players, etc. That would be a good minimum to grow from if we are forced to teach students that do not care about our particular subject. If the motivation fails every time, we can still be content about the passive knowledge reaching them if only at a fraction of what they would learn if they were invested in the class. Ultimately, the process of transmission of knowledge is not the sole responsibility of the teacher, it's good to remember that.

c) The teaching environment can be improved significantly to the point where a mediocre teacher can achieve better results than a better one. Teaching inside a construction site full of noises with dozens of people locked in a room struggling for air, etc. can decrease the efficiency significantly. Let's imagine that I didn't know much about medieval warfare but I had to teach you some of it to you. Having replicas of weapons and armors available, as well as 3D projections of battlefields, maps, and armies in a correctly ventilated room with plants to purify the air, windows, perfect light that allows people to concentrate, etc. would keep increasing my final results against the most knowledgeable scholar in the noisy construction site from the previous example. Air quality has a deep effect in cognitive performance. Comfortable chairs can increase the attention and stamina of the students. Environmental factors can therefore improve our performance dramatically. Keeping good materials, updated preparations, trying to anticipate the doubts and questions of the students based on current events and past experience, and using technological advances ends up having a deep effect on the whole teaching process.

d) The teaching methods vary according to the subjects, the context, and even the students. It's good to have different alternatives available, even after we found the best ones for us. In other words: our teaching methodology has to be flexible and include less-common options for those specific cases where we need to deviate from the habits that have worked for us so far. Teaching children instead of adults, people without an ample previous educational background, people with disabilities, subjects that require practical applications of theoretical methods, etc. All those unexpected circumstances we can find in our lives are faced with more chances of success if we are ready to adapt our methodology to the circumstances in order to favor the final results. Something very important about the teaching methodologies we can find is the fact that some of them were created just as an exercise in futility: "look! I created a new way to teach you the Norwegian language with sock puppets and songs!" Yes, good for you as a creative mind, but is this new method better in terms of performance and results? Will this allow me to teach more and faster? Or was it just a useless display of creativity that will have no real impact on my teaching abilities?

e) The institution. Although teaching is an activity we will all have to perform in one degree or another throughout our lives, sometimes we need to do so as part of some established institution: an academy, a university, a high school, etc. In these cases it's important to determine if the rules and protocols in place allow us to perform our duties. It may seem something basic, but a lot of people who identify teaching with the concept of a profession can't really tell when they are being restricted to the point where they can no longer perform adequately. Instead of identifying the defects of the institutional approach, they will blame themselves for the shortcomings of the final results. Getting burnt-out is a real danger when one teaches for some time if we don't identify the correct parameters and goals of the activity we are performing. If you are forced to teach a difficult class at 7.00 am, if the students can lack discipline without consequences, or if you are not granted enough control over the teaching process you can end up being set up for failure.

f) Balancing sciences, arts, physical activities, and humanities. Whatever you are teaching, it helps to keep in mind what is being done in other areas to realize if you are deviating too much from common parameters. If you are teaching languages with games and attitudes that would be unthinkable in a math class, if you are teaching a sport without providing any reference or material where the students could learn more, if you are teaching some system or science without allowing for the experimentation and free-thinking attitudes of other subjects, in all these cases it would be good to consider balancing out the methodologies if we suspect that the results could be improved.

Teaching has allowed me to learn more about myself and all that, but following the main subject of this book, I can't say it has taken me anywhere transcendental in the end. I started teaching (as a profession) at 21 or so. Private classes, language companies, high schools, universities in different countries... but even nowadays when a student asks me something about the future I must admit that I am as lost as they are. Instead of providing some light for the way I join them and admit that being a good teacher was another one of those dreams that I thought would fulfill me spiritually, or at a human level, but it hasn't. It's particularly problematic because due to my specializations I have to teach future generations of teachers. I can teach the skills, the theory, share practical cases, show them the relevant research in pedagogy, etc. but as soon as we enter the field of motivation, fulfillment, vocational stuff, and all that I have to be honest with them. I am not sure I have found my place in the world 16 years after I first started in this activity.

It could be considered as a lack of spiritual connection with life, or a circumstantial limitation in my perception from overcoming obstacle after obstacle without really achieving meaningful victories, but I suspect I am not the only one who keeps doing things well and not reaching that sense of peace and fulfillment that is supposed to accompany a victory or a triumph. In many ways it feels a lot like winning a battle and hastily preparing for the next one that will be a bit more difficult and unfulfilling than the last one. Achieving for nothing.

jolly character merrily strolling around "Hey! Cheer up mate! You are bringing everybody down! Life is beautiful and challenges help us learn and improve and keeping positive is always better than frowning and crying in a corner!" Yes, I know the theory as well as anyone else. The world is indeed full of beautiful meadows and waterfalls, and children that open their Christmas presents full of joy, and couples who fall in love and all that. We know, we know... The topic of the discussion now is not about looking at the bright side of things. We can do that while at the same time analyzing the things that are not right, fair, or performing at optimal levels. We have all experienced moments of happiness and moments of sadness, but the neutral state of "being" or "existing" needs to be optimized in each of us to be on the positive side of a vital balance that so often tends towards the negative consequences.

Happiness without an honest base would be a lie. Repeating myself that I have reached many goals I set myself to achieve and therefore I should be happy would be an empty exercise in self-deception. Doesn't it make more sense to analyze life from an objective and impartial point of view and try to find out what we are lacking? What we can change? What needs to be done differently? Am I living in the right place for me? Should I be doing something else with my life? Something more meaningful and personal? I truly belief those are the questions that I can pose myself while still trying to be positive and as happy as one can be under the current circumstances. So that's how I decided it would be good to let others know that you are not alone in your endless quest for happiness, meaning, and fulfillment. I am not here to tell you to put on a happy face. I am here to sit down with you and nod... yep... I am as lost as you are and I can only feel a bit happier to make you company, if only with my written words... I won that game, I defended myself in that fight, I graduated from that thing, I got that job, I kissed that special person, I traveled to that place... and I still feel myself as lost as when I was a child. Things keep happening, I keep doing my best, and instead of being the titan I imagined I would be I am still going around wondering what can I do to make myself, others, and the world a bit happier... keeping in mind that there is a risk that even if I achieve that goal it may have also been for nothing, like all the rest. And even with that prospect in mind, I try to be as positive as I can. Why? Because even in the event that life is pointless, it would be pointless for the bad and for the good alike. Problems also lose their importance in the vast scheme of the universe once we finish the game and we go to that peaceful light, which takes me to the next chapter.

CHAPTER SEVEN: Spirituality and Deep stuff

We have to hold two ideas at the same time. They are complementary, not contradictory. On the one hand we have the life we are experiencing and our feeling of being immersed in it. On the other hand we have the spiritual experience that takes a new shape after dying.

Let's say your personal beliefs point you in the direction that there is nothing after you die. Improbable as it may be, that would also be some sort of spiritual experience. A consciousness that disappears and atoms that go back to the initial source of matter. It is in itself something else; something beyond this life.

However, I am one of those who thinks there is much, much more after this life of ours. The example I tend to use for the mindset in which I place my spirituality is something along the lines of entering a room where there is a rope connected to a bowling ball, that would push some dominoes to fall in a chain reaction to move a hammer that hits some lever, pushing another ball to fall in a basket, etc. "What will happen next? Come on! Tell me if you are so smart!" I have no idea what will happen in the next 27, 43, or 86 steps in this room I have entered but I naturally tend to mistrust two kinds of people: The ones who tell me there is nothing to see in that room, and that it's all a series of coincidences without any further purpose... and the ones who claim to know everything that will happen at every move with absolute certainty until the glorious end.

I am able to join the dots, follow the clues, and come to the conclusion that there is more to life than just living it and dying. I can see noble feelings in animals, as well as brutal chaos. I can see dolphins helping sailors who fall overboard without anything to gain from it, and I can also see how they rape the females of their species in a group sometimes: the best and the worst in one species of animal. I can see how everything seems designed to test us, challenge us, and make us overcome difficulties... I honestly believe we would be growing and learning more from neutral experiences and positive ones than from empty suffering, and artificial challenges, but it's also true that there could be many different explanations for that particular circumstance. We come to this world with innocence and purity of heart in most of the cases, so it seems logical to assume that we come from a place that has those qualities in abundance, or that this would be our normal state of existence. However can one be truly GOOD by choice without the ability to do evil? Can we examine our true goodness of nature and embrace it without having seen with our own eyes a place where that goodness coexists with destructive forces and negative impulses? So that could very well be an element that is important in this equation. Everything seems too skewed to the side of endless personal human improvement. Even when you want to abandon yourself in a quiet place, life seems to find ways to test you and annoy you with more problems and challenges to solve.

So there is a mystery surrounding us and we lack pieces of the puzzle to complete it beyond any semblance of doubt, but it seems pretty obvious if you pay attention that the puzzle indeed exists, and the parameters of it defy statistics for random chaotic events. Some vital stories seem to be scripted in convoluted ways that fail the test of sampling. This phenomenon can be observed in historical cases. There are biographies out there that defy the most elementary connection with the general state of things. In other words: I have no idea if we choose parts of our lives and circumstances before coming to Earth at the precise time we do, but even in the deepest most secretive mysteries you can't blur patterns or escape observation and statistical analysis. Our human intelligence gives us a few powers like these that we often disregard. We are vulnerable and feeble creatures in the great scheme of things, but we sure seem good at identifying patterns and picking up on odd details that don't make sense. Let's take one example: Violet Jessop, the woman that survived the sinking of the Titanic, and then again the sinking of the Britannic, and yet again the sinking of the Olympic. We can calculate the odds of three big ships sinking, the same person being on board the three of them, and the same person managing to save her life on the three occasions. We could play those odds against the list of maritime disasters happening in the first period of the 20th century, then select the disasters that happen by countries, maritime companies, etc. We also have to take into account the fact that Violet was working as part of the crew in those ships to be precise and accurate, but in any case, take a look at the list of big ships that sunk in those years and tell me if participating in (and surviving) three disasters with similar circumstances isn't something suspicious.

I am not saying that we can cherry-pick things here and there to support a theory. That's precisely what conspiracy theories are all about. They take useful things for their narrative, ignore the rest, they link it all together, and human beings hungry for finding sense in madness and chaos accept those theories as correct. In this case we are taking raw facts, comparing them against general trends, and concluding that there is a statistical anomaly that might indicate foul play in tampering with the regular odds of things happening. If you don't agree with this particular thought of mine it's ok, I can also help with that: Remember that women and children were given priority when leaving a sinking ship, so saving your life might have been easier as a woman working in that ship than as a male passenger. Shifts were also different back then so maybe that lady was working non-stop without alternating with others that might have occupied her position the days those ships sunk. One more detail to disprove this particular case may be the fact that the three ships she was in had been designed by the same company, so they were "sister ships" and there may have been flaws in those designs. Why undermining my own theory? Because I am seeking for the truth, so everything needs to be perfectly accurate. I am not looking to validate an existing idea, but rather to describe how analyzing historical anomalies makes me sometimes think stuff along the lines of: "wait a minute... let me check how that defies statistics and odds... well, well, well... It would seem as if someone was designing a personal and tailored adventure here on Earth and forgot that simply by doing things differently from others we can see the discrepancies from what random chance would provide as a result".

There are many historical coincidences out there that reinforce my idea that perhaps the original design for this reality might have fooled those who didn't have access to information about everything that's going on in the rest of the world. With more data, comes more knowledge... the knowledge that in turn allows us to see odd movements that seem artificial and out of the realm of random events. What do I do with this information? I combine it with the suspicion that the mechanisms in this world seem to favor our development, and furthermore I use my own instincts: I am not at home here. This doesn't feel like my place or perhaps not my time, so that opens a few options. These would include the possibility that I have chosen to be here on my own in order to gain certain experiences that would benefit me in my development from the point of view that this is not my natural environment. Some sort of existential tourist if you will. The second option would be that I (we) might be visiting this type of life for the first time, be it as some sort of spiritual demotion, be it as some sort of intermediate step to decide who goes where from here. Even if you and I were natives to Earth from past lives, our existence in a peaceful fishing village, or in a primitive community from thousands of years ago might still not make us feel that we belong here. Same planet, same type of human creature, but a totally different environment that makes us feel external to it all.

One more option closely related with some of the points I have addressed before would be the possibility that I have no control over the type of life I am living here, even assuming that the desire to come was entirely mine and I wasn't forced into it. That would also explain the reticence and the resentment to most of the negative things that are not part of my nature. In those options we could fit the statistical anomalies even if we need to work with different hypothetical scenarios at once. You either designed this type of life experience for yourself, or it was designed for you for reasons beyond certainty, that would probably have to do with an interest in particular life experiences that can be found here and now. That would be the raw logic, now I am going to speculate without footholds of any kind: Spartans were separated from their parents as children to put them under the tutelage of the state. All of the Spartan children, so if my particular flavor of life experience had to be "losing your parents while everyone around you seems to stay normal and only you are in that position" being born in Sparta would have been useless if you find comfort in the military system together with hundreds of other boys in your situation. A war wouldn't have done the trick either. Lots of British children in WW2 talk about the times of Chronicles of Narnia when they were sent away from the cities and all that. Again, all of them had that situation and could find comfort in each other. In the times of Oliver Twist personal tragedies related to the loss of a parent would have been quite common. So if the particular taste you want is "personal loss of a parent, then another, feeling alone in the world while everyone else stays more or less normal with their life stories" you would need to select a particular time without wars, catastrophes, so that there aren't 27 other kids in your same situation with whom you can play and enjoy, therefore altering the life experience.

With this framework in mind, and considering we need free will to make the choices and make use of life as a learning tool (meaning, that we aren't predetermined to act in certain ways, just provided the setting and circumstances where we must do whatever we want) we can also deduct that interfering for good would be positive, but interfering for the worst would be counterproductive. Allow me to elaborate. Helping someone at some point we might be diminishing the impact of his personal vital needs, but universal solidarity might also be the thing he came here to experience. We sail uncharted waters with those possibilities, although I side with helping being good for us since it makes us happy at a deep level. It's as if we are equipped with mechanisms that act as a compass for those things: "I am helping someone, I am the savior, I am a positive power in this world... I feel well by helping!" It's not the same mechanism as when we eat junk food and it feels well at a superficial level, but deep inside we know it's actually bad to abuse such food every day, for example.

However, negative actions upon others might be disruptive at a level beyond our comprehension. Our free will allows us to perform actions whose consequences require too much brain power to predict, brain power that we do not possess as humans. So whenever an organization or individual wants to perform negative actions to further a good cause I always assume they are too stupid to know what they are doing. Predicting consequences when so many variables are unknown is more like gambling with your soul and the life stories of others at incredibly complex levels... A recipe for failures of dramatic consequences. So let's take an example for this: Henry Tandey, a war hero from WW1 (the most decorated one apparently) that decided not to shoot Adolf at some point where he could have killed him during that conflict. It's the type of scenario where it's easy to get confused and end up losing your soul... Any scenario that has to do with killing Adolf before he did any of the things he did in WW2. Germany was deeply humiliated after the peace treaties and reparations for losing WW1, the situation was ripe for anyone to drive them to war a second time because they couldn't really function as a country under those conditions. Imagine if WW2 happens with a different leadership but a few years later. We could have had a conflict with nuclear weapons... if you remember, they appeared just a few years after the end of the war. The scientists would have still been alive, the research would have had more years to be complete, but instead of some dumb corporal losing battle after battle you might have had German efficiency and someone like Rommel calling the shots in the battlefields of Europe or Russia. The anti-Semitic environment would have still been there, and most of the worst ideas and plans came from other people and not directly from the top. So if someone actually went back in time and killed baby Adolf or something like that, he would have just doomed the world to a big-scale military conflict where Germany would have had better weapons, better leadership, and would have probably won the war. Surely the opposite of the original idea.

The same logic can be applied for most organizations and political parties that have supposedly good goals, but with the small problem that to get to their dreamland of utopian happiness some unethical or unfair decisions should be taken. It's mesmerizing to see how I am terrified of the unexpected consequences and repercussions of my small-scale actions, and yet you can see throughout history people affecting millions of lives without the slightest knowledge of what they are doing or being able to predict even a small fraction of all the ripple effects their actions would cause. As a general rule, I deeply mistrust people who claim we can be better human beings in the future, after we are done committing evil atrocities in the present, then everything will be fine and those horrible injustices will be forgotten and blah, blah. It shocks me that so many people can fall for that trap of the end justifying the means, or the evil actions of today being washed away by the utopian glories of tomorrow's "greater good". It's not intellectually accurate because evil and horror don't work in scales. This is what I mean... We could commit some unethical action if that action doesn't compromise our overall integrity. Something mildly unethical could be indeed overshadowed by some amazing positive outcome, but those concepts don't work in scales, so killing some innocent person to save five other people with his/her organs would still make someone a horrible despicable killer... Prolonging five lives by sacrificing an innocent person is astronomically far from balancing anything even if that philosophical concept were indeed correct, which it isn't.

So every time I see some conspiracy theory (not because there aren't accurate ones, I am referring to the fake ones now) claiming that a bunch of individuals got together to share common goals, agreed on measures to be carried out, and those measures are unethical... I usually sigh deeply and begin to explain how social groups work, dissent theories, factions within a group, and most importantly: How incredibly difficult it is for an intelligent person to be brainwashed into believing that wildly unethical actions can produce long-term positive results in the big scheme of things. It's one of those concepts that goes against the most essential logic: "Look at this beautiful park! Look at all those children enjoying it! We built it on top of a sacred cemetery after kicking the owners out and destroying the graves..." Aha, great, now you are making oblivious children and their families accomplices of your lack of ethical intelligence. "Timmy! Remember the park where I used to take you? Well let me tell you how we came to enjoy that park". And then Timmy will exchange a happy childhood memory for a guilty conscience. And no, I am not saying that Timmy is indeed responsible for the actions of his predecessors, nor am I advocating for inherited blame or anything like that. I am simply stating that our childhood memories would be soured by the knowledge of horrible injustices being committed upon others just so that we could be slightly happier.

So going further into the subject of what's after this life, and all that, I can say that although it is a bit difficult to work with deductions, incomplete information, and examples that may or may not be true depending on the case-by-case methodology and the circumstances, it would be wiser to suspect the existence of a system in place, governed by external powers and mechanisms that may not even need to be personified in deities to make sense. We have a lot of noise mixed with the data when it comes to spiritual beliefs and theories that have historical roots. Logic is a good way to determine what makes sense and what doesn't. So taking for example Buddhism, when Siddhartha explains that you need to experience for yourself, that meditation is better than inflicting pain on your body, or that once you reach some truth you need to share it with others to fulfill your sacred duties, that part sounds logical and accurate. When in the middle of the story yellow dragons appear in the sky and the guy rips his eyelids and a plum tree begins to grow and all that nonsense, the wisdom of the text drops so significantly that it is pretty obvious which parts were written by a wise man, and which parts were written by a dumb monk decades later to try and impress simple-minded people who weren't grasping the main concept explained to them: "Well... you are supposed to do good things to increase the positive effects of your presence in this planet, together with meditation for peace of mind and knowing yourself and your past lives and... wait don't go! You know what? After that dragons appear and shiunnn! shiunnn! Magic trees! Fireworks!"

Brahmanism tells us that we are all part of a bigger entity. A universe experiencing itself through the division of its whole into smaller parts. It could make sense to think we are all connected. Even if this belief turns out not to be true, it's interesting that people 4,000 years ago were able to come up with such complex theories about existence. It seems to point in the direction that it would be unwise to dismiss their spiritual beliefs as plain wrong and that's it. As soon as I see logic and common sense in places where you wouldn't expect to find it, it makes me cautious and interested. Shintoism has a special element of communion with nature and appreciation for the place where you live and the beauty it has to offer that is also very sensible. We do seem happier when nature offers us beauty. It's like a fascination for the wonders this world has to present, and although humans have created many beautiful things, nature appeals to our primal instincts and our most essential sense of awe and inspiration.

One of the mechanisms I use to select the validity of beliefs is an effective variety of confirmation bias (if there is such a thing). What I mean is that sometimes you feel some things related to friendship, love, death, the purpose of life, etc. and suddenly you realize that someone centuries ago already thought about these things and arrived to some interesting conclusions that seem to be in agreement with yours and even expand upon them. Having a bias is rarely a good idea, but this kind of double-check for beliefs and philosophical theories has proven very useful to me throughout the years. The danger is that some people might be telling me what I want to hear to make me feel well, so that's when critical thinking comes into effect. I enjoy having my beliefs and ideas properly challenged. Accurate criticism is like a chisel that keeps taking away inaccuracies and wrong concepts from the general truth so that it becomes pure and without imperfections.

I often catch myself torn between wishing for a life with love and happiness, and at the same time afraid that the love of my life and soulmate has to be in this awful reality with me for that. To see her get older, sick, and die or to let her see me going through the same and leaving her alone for a few years. It's hard when that happens with people you love... it would be devastating with the person you will ever love the most. So in a way I am satisfied with doing whatever needs to be done in this life alone, dating nice girls knowing perfectly well they are not "the one", and waiting for the moment in which I can finally stare at the divinity and explain that I wasn't comfortable here, that this was not my place, that I never let myself go, that I never became one of them, and that I have witnessed things that shouldn't exist. And when they answer that hardship makes us learn and evolve I will calmly explain that I learned much more in the moments and situations when I was comfortable, happy, and safe... because I may not know much about the intricacies of the universe, but I do know enough about teaching and learning to prove to any higher power that Earth is not the right way as it stands.

Did I ever consider ending my life when I was a teenager or further on in life? Never seriously... I thought about the concept and agreed that it would be justified to avoid torture, being eaten by wild animals, a painful incurable illness, and stuff like that. The most I would do is pursuing dangerous activities that don't have an impact on my health if I stay alive. So for example at some points in my life it was easy seeing me swimming in dangerous sea waters with huge waves, not wanting to die, obviously, but as a new door that opens when you can take more risks. If nothing happens you had a fun afternoon, and if you drown it's not really suiciding because you played it safe and didn't have that intention, just embraced that possibility of an extra risk. Why so technical about this subject? Because I do believe it would be something I would need to justify since it's disruptive for my life narrative and for the universe. Quitting the game is rarely the way to win. Remember before when I mentioned that we don't know the repercussions or consequences of our negative actions? Well killing a person is a negative action even if that person is myself, so I would feel like an idiot if after standing defiant in the face of this crazy life for years and years I ended it all and then the conversation with the light went like: "Erm... You were supposed to keep teaching others, living a lonely life, and at 73 years old saving the future father of a little girl from falling down a rail... That girl would be your future loved one in your next reincarnation and now we can't make you experience a pleasant version of Earth... You didn't die a hero, you just quit before your time... You spoiled everything for yourself by your own hand".

That last conversation could be going a million different ways for a million different reasons, but the point still stands... Abandoning a tennis match because of how hard it is, or because of the public booing a player would mean losing the match. Abandoning a tennis match because you broke a leg and a piece of bone perforated some artery and blah, blah, is something logical that can be justified. The authorities can be in trouble if they don't stop the match themselves actually. Just to be clear, I am not saying that breaking a leg is a cause for ending it all... that would be dumb. I am saying that if the Mongols of Genghis Khan torture their prisoners for days and you happen to have lost a battle against them in the 13th century, you could end it all after ensuring all your other options are depleted. If after that some divinity explained you that the Mongols would have kept you as a translator and not harm you, you could claim the high risks involved in making that gamble. So no, the loss of my parents, the stress of life, and all those other things are not enough to justify direct action... It would literally have to be something related to physical pain, imminent, and without alternatives no matter how cray they are. Moving is always an option, starting in a new place, getting a new job somewhere else, etc. And I think there is something I like about going on living: It makes the universe be in my debt, at least in this life. Allow me to elaborate: If you do your best to be a good person, to not harm others, to be a positive influence, and all that... and the universe keeps giving you hardships, pain, and things you don't deserve... The universe is in your debt. Justice has not been respected in your case. You behave better than life, so you are superior to it, above it... of higher benefit and quality in general terms; a force for good. If life and you were neighbors and I had to choose who I want in the house next door I would choose you, and life would be the crazy psycho that goes around throwing salt in people's gardens, and answering good morning greetings with grunts and evil glares...

So yes, there is some inherent value in being above the circumstances you happen to live, in standing your ground saying: "No, wait, wait... I want to see how far the imbalance between what I give and what I receive from life can go..." I want to be able to point at all those examples when after I die they try to convince me that hardship and suffering build character and all that. I imagine it like some sort of cosmic trial where regardless of how advanced those beings are, you can point at the vastly unfair examples and shame them into acceptance. Like a puppy who could suddenly talk and had to go against the best defense lawyer on Earth: "Honorable members of the jury, the defendant kicked me repeatedly in the face as he laughed and claimed -I hate puppies! Suffer! Suffer! Mwhahahahahah! There are plenty of witnesses, video footage, and the defendant admitted 5 times during the trial that making puppies suffer helped them build character or something of that sort". And then the defense lawyer would be like: "Errr... hum... Well... You see, my client is not mentally fit and we throw ourselves at the jury's mercy". And then after the trial: "Puppy! Some words about the ruling today?" "Yes, yes... This is a great day for puppies worldwide. Kicking us in the face claiming it's for our own good needs to stop, and hopefully the universe can correct itself after this victory today. A great day for universal justice. Thank you very much". Change puppies for human beings, kicks in the face for life suffering beyond balance, and the crazy puppy-kicker for whoever or whatever is running this version of life, existence, or reality, and you got yourself an amazing trial so I like the idea of going prepared into it with plenty of examples to crush even the best cosmic lawyers out there: "How can there be toddlers with cancer? What type of valuable lesson is worth all that suffering for everyone involved? A tsunami comes and kills hundreds of people in Asia... Where is the valuable lesson to be learned? And if they all needed to die cause it was their time, what about the mental distress you cause to those who deem it a random act of nature without logic?" *points his cosmic finger* "I accuse the creators and rulers of this version of existence of being unfair, unbalanced, cruel in pain, mild in happiness, and of committing abuses of power against the will of the beings involved under their dealings. Furthermore! I accuse them of being less able of impartiality and justice than some of the beings they are supposed to be developing, for even us down here would make a better version of existence where everyone could develop better and more efficiently without all those horrible and appalling mechanisms that serve for nothing but to bring shame and injustice upon those who put the system in place, and those who see the effects this system produces and having the power and ability to improve it, they don't". And that's the thing about reason, justice, fairness, logic... It doesn't really matter if there is a superior being incredibly more powerful and intelligent than you are, if you are right in your description of the facts and circumstances that are producing an unfair existence.

Why am I so sure that the spiritual life has logic and justice? Because otherwise it would make human beings the superior creatures in existence. Think about it logically. If you or I are better judges of what is right and what is wrong than those powers placed above us in the system, we would actually be subject to a double injustice. As if we took away the engineers and architects that build our cities or bridges, replaced them with barbers and then we saw the structures collapse while we talk about suffering to develop character and blah, blah. And for the final argument that some people seem to have about humans being the ones that make this world as it is, I throw upon you the abused rights of the minority together with the unfairness of collective guilt and punishments: Let's assume we belong to the group "humans", we would also belong to the subgroup "humans who are not being treated fairly by life", so effectively we would be a minority whose rights are not being represented nor respected. If someone wants to punish "humans" it could only be possible to do so using collective guilt as an excuse, since there are subgroups of humans that do not deserve such hardships and pains. The subgroup of humans under the abuse of an unfair life system deserves a justice that is not being bestowed upon them, so even assuming that we are going to a better existence after this one, the injustices inflicted upon us wouldn't wash away

even if we ourselves wished it to be so. The crimes don't
disappear just because the victim agrees not to pursue the
matter after the payment of a better life has been agreed upon.

I guess that by now you may be wondering why I seemed so
negative at the beginning if now I seem to have a very rich inner
world and all that. The truth is that both concepts can be true at
once. I can enjoy teaching and doubt the deep meaning of what I
teach. I can figure out some important yet small parts of the
mysteries of life applying logic, reasoning, and heart... and yet I
still have to fulfill my life with all the challenges that
accumulate one after another. Sometimes we will be more
connected to others, and sometimes it will seem that we are
alone. The truth seems to be a mixture in balance because
although we are connected by our ideas and experiences being
lived in this planet we call Earth, it is also true that I lack the
ability and the power to help you and be there for you... and that
hurts me for reasons that escape cultural habits. I don't know
who you are, but the fact that you have been reading my deepest
thoughts, fears, and ideas somehow connects us at a universal
level. We don't need to know each other personally to agree that
it is an honor for me to share or have shared this planet with you
depending on the year in which you are reading this. I hope you
and I can both find our way, and I say this sitting there with you,
as lost as you are, but happy that we could be connected in this
way. Thank you for being there for me, as I am here for you. Do
the best you can knowing that it is always hard for people like
you and me. And above all, don't make me lack your existence
until it is the right time for you and for me to leave this world.
Thank you for everything you do.

THE END